Crossing the Borderline

Crossing the Borderline

By

Jennifer Khoh

A TRUE STORY ADAPTED FROM A JOURNAL WRITTEN AT AGE NINE

The names of some characters in my story have been changed in consideration of individual privacy.

ISBN 978-0-9834206-0-6

For orders contact:

Purple Leaf Publishing

P.O. Box 15062

Oklahoma City, OK 73155

Contents

Part I

The Unexpected Journey

Chapter 1

England

The simple act of persuasion that a person is capable of unleashing is immense. Some individuals affect a single person, while others affect an entire population. Be it the former or the latter, they have an impact. In 1975, a select few were stepping forward, altering the shape of the future. Margaret Thatcher became the leader of the Conservative Party in England, inspiring women all across England to reaffirm their freedom and once again cast their brassieres to the wind. In the United States, Bill Gates was founding Microsoft, laying the path for ordinary citizens to become computer literate, changing the world as we know it. On a more personal level, during that same year, Elizabeth Bing, my mother, devised a plan that influenced and transformed my perception of life forever. It didn't affect the whole world in a big way, but it did change me. A decision so seemingly inconsequential led to a most dramatic, life-changing experience.

A cold winter day in February 1975 marked the beginning of events that transformed my life forever. I had recently turned nine years old, and I wanted to listen to some records that I had received for my birthday. My thirteen-year-old sister, Jane, loved music. She was the bearer of the record player. Upon my request, she removed the rocking T. Rex single that was playing and placed one of my new vinyl records on the turntable. She carefully balanced the stylus on the edge of the shiny black disc as I eagerly waited for the new music to start. Setting up the record player was a tricky ordeal, so I hardly ever opted to do it myself. The few times I did try, my shaky hand ended up scratching a record or ruining the stylus, so I was happy to let Jane set up the music for me. After a few clicking sounds, the song finally began. We sat on the soft carpet in our bedroom, listening to Donny Osmond sing his hit "Puppy Love." Our own beloved puppy, Katie, lay curled up comfortably on a cushion placed next to my bed. As I listened to the music and petted Katie's raggedy black coat, I felt a presence over my shoulder like I was being watched.

It was Mother lurking in the hallway. When she entered the room, immediately I thought that we had made too much noise, and I watched her body language, waiting for a reaction. Jane quickly stopped the music. I watched carefully as my mother stood in the entry, one hand on the door frame and the other perched on her hip. Long pieces of dark auburn hair stuck out of her scarf in an unruly manner. Even from where I was sitting, I could see Mother's mesmerizing green eyes sparkling in the bright lighting in our room as if they were alive and independent from the body that they adorned. Her creamy white skin was flushed, as though she had been doing some severe spring cleaning. Something was amiss. Fixated on the eyes that were Mother's focal point, I expected to hear the usual parental demand for silence, a plea to release her from the burden of child sounds that gave her great pain in the form of migraines that lasted for days. The look on Jane's face told me that she felt the same vibe, but instead of reprimanding us, Mother had an announcement to make that had nothing to do with loud music or headaches.

By now Katie was off her cushion and standing with her tongue hanging out the side of her snout, her tail wagging furiously like she was interested in what Mother had to say. Jovially, Mother declared that we were moving. I knew something was different about her: she was too happy, and more lively than usual. I sat motionless, waiting for the rest of the announcement. Overenthusiastically she informed Jane and me that we were not simply relocating to a new house in the neighborhood or to a nearby city; we were moving to Australia. I didn't know much about the country, only that it was "down under" somewhere. I wasn't sure what had contributed to her decision, either. Maybe it was the cold English weather, or possibly it was because most of our extended family had already emigrated to warmer climates. More than likely, though, being equipped with her distinctive and capricious nature, she had just determined that she needed a change. I found that to be somewhat strange, because our family life appeared to be cheerful and content. Apart from the inconsequential marital spats between Mother and my step-father Ryan, there was no indication that our lifestyle was unhappy, unhealthy, or dysfunctional. For the first time in a while, everything was going relatively well. We had a pleasant home, comfort, and security. Evidently, it was too cozy. Mother presumably felt that our life had become mundane and monotonous. Whatever the reason for the decision, the news was completely random, out of the blue. Mother was always a little eccentric and unpredictable, but this outdid anything else so far. For a split second I thought that maybe she was joking, but I knew better than to voice that question. If Mother said something was going to happen, it was, and nothing anyone else had to say would change her mind, especially children. I learned at a very young age that children were to be silent and not speak unless spoken to directly. Talking back was an absolute no-no. Consequently I was a very quiet and somewhat shy child. Jane's voice was the communication between my mother and me, but this time she wasn't saying anything.

The next day, there was to be a family discussion around the dinner table regarding the move. Ryan had not arrived yet, so I sat quietly playing with the red ribbon on the end of one of my long brown pigtails, which protruded unevenly on each side of my head due to my own attempts at grooming. I kept on moving the ribbon away from my face as far as the braid would take it and back again, which caused me to cross my eyes every time it was close to my nose. Mother was quick to stop me from entertaining myself, explaining how my eyes would stay stuck in the cross-eyed position forever if I didn't stop. Jane sat opposite me, rolling her huge brown eyes and huffing away at her newly cut hair, which left her bangs dropping into her face. She chewed furiously on a three-hour piece of gum she had in her mouth. Mother abruptly stopped that behavior too. This time the reason was lockjaw. If Jane kept on chewing gum, she would get lockjaw, whatever that was. Jane was not amused by the situation at all and began pushing Katie with her foot; the dog was trying to sleep comfortably under the table. That was obviously a ploy to take the boredom out of the incredibly long wait for the inevitable family talk.

Finally Ryan entered. His lanky frame was hunched over slightly, and his blond hair hung around his face, perfectly framing his trimmed sideburns, mustache, and beard. He had a depressed look about him, as though he were about to be put in front of a firing squad. He sat down at the end of the table, and the conversation began. It was more of a lecture than a discussion, as no one but Mother had anything to say. Mostly the details of the move were covered in the talk. At no time were any of us asked if we wanted to move—not even Ryan. He usually had a laid-back, anything-goes kind of attitude, but it was very apparent that this change made him concerned.

Initially, the announcement was received with anything but enthusiasm. I was against leaving England, because I was training to be a figure skater and future Olympic Gold medalist. That was my goal in life. I retained the same Bristol Ice Rink coach as Robin Cousins, who went on to become the Winter Olympic champion in 1980. My sister was reluctant to move, as she had been accepted at one of Bristol's highly esteemed girls' schools. Plus, she would miss all her friends, and she had a lot of them. Ryan was opposed to the idea too, because he didn't want to leave his parents and brother. They lived in London, about one hundred and twenty miles from where we lived in Bristol, and even that was too far away for him. But when my mother had an "inspirational idea," it was set in stone. Mother assured me that Australia had ice rinks, so I could continue on with my dream; she told Jane that the country had good schools and that she would soon make new friends; and Ryan was informed that England was just an airport away from anywhere in the world. Mother convinced us all that the move would be a success. It was all good—for her, anyway. It didn't make sense to me why we were making this big change, but nothing ever made any sense when it came to the decisions Mother made.

Within four weeks, all of the arrangements for the excursion had been completed. Visas and passport applications were processed, approved, and received. The apartment, complete with furnishings, was sold, adding to Mother's savings for the move; and Katie, our much-loved pet, was headed to a new home with my Uncle Seward. Our brand-new four-door Datsun Sunny was traded in for a 1968 Volkswagen van; that was another unforeseen event. We loved the family car.

Looking back, it was hard to believe that she would ever trade in that car. The day Mother came home with Sunny, she was so proud and happy. It was the first brand-new car she had ever bought. It was a sign of good fortune for us. She had come running into the house and gathered Jane and me to take a ride down to the local shopping area. She wanted to parade our new arrival around town. Having a car was not just a convenience; it was a sign of prosperity or at least a show of stability, something that had not existed for us until she married Ryan and moved to Bristol. They both had good jobs and had been working hard to save money, and now we had a car to show for their work. As we drove down the high road, I had noticed the smile on Mother's face. It was so nice to see her happy, as much of the time she appeared upset or distracted. That day it was different. It felt good to know that she felt good. We had parked on the road near a Tesco grocery store where we were going to shop. As we were exiting the new car, a raggedy old woman came up to us. She was from the gypsy camp that had been set up by the river near where we lived. She approached Mother and in a mysterious, croaky voice asked her to cross her palm with a silver coin. I was a little apprehensive about this person and hung close to my mother's side. The woman reminded me of the wicked witch in the *Snow White* movie, which I'd recently been lucky to see in the movie theater. The old woman looked at me with a crooked smile full of rotten teeth. Then she said, "You fear me, child? I am the least of your worries, for the future brings fears beyond your little imagination." She cut off with a weird laugh and held out her hand to my mother, repeating the silver coin line. She scared me. Reluctantly my mother placed a one-pound note in the woman's hand. With lightning speed, the pound disappeared into a purse hanging around the old woman's waist, and she grabbed my mother's hand and proceeded to supposedly tell her fortune by the lines on her hands. "I see … a long journey in your future, one that will bring about many changes. You will be leaving all your worldly possessions behind, and you will—" Before the woman could finish her reading, my mother pulled back her hand, thanked the woman, grabbed Jane and me, and ran off down the street, away from the creepy old gypsy. As we sped away, I heard more words from the gypsy's mouth: something about a curse. When we finally entered Tesco, my mother was rambling on about how ridiculous the woman was, saying that we had settled for almost four years and just bought a new car, and that she was never going to part with or leave our precious home. She was noticeably upset about the reading, and the usual distant look returned to her face. It made me sad to think she had been happy before that sinister old hag had spoken to her.

Anyway, I never knew whether the gypsy's talk had influenced my mother to go to Australia, but one thing I did know was we were going on a journey to a distant land, and Sunny was gone. I thought it was going to be shipped to Australia at a later date, but apparently not. It seemed silly to be so emotionally attached to a vehicle, but it seemed more than just metal and glass with wheels. Mother had given it a personality when she brought it home and told us that it was a Sunny. I asked her why she called it that. She said it was because on sunny days we could take day trips in it, and we did. On day trips to the seaside or to quaint little farm towns in England, Mother would put a tape in the eight-track, usually the Shadows or the Beach Boys, and we would sing all the way to wherever it was we were going. Sunny had sentimental value. "Sunny" was the model of the car, but since it was associated with sunny weekend outings, we just called it that. I was upset that Mother had traded it in for a van, but it was part of her plan for us.

Being totally unconventional, my mother decided that not only were we moving to the other side of the world, which was thousands of miles away from home, across numerous countries and large bodies of water, but we would also make an adventure out of it. We would be driving over land most of the way in the van. The vehicle, purchased for the sole purpose of serving Mother's spontaneous desire to move, was so much more than I had imagined, but not in a good way. It was an ugly, olive green, older Volkswagen model that was customized for camping and traveling long distances. It was secondhand, but it ran well on the test drive, so as far as my mother was concerned, it was a done deal. This was going to be our best friend for the next few weeks—up close and personal. Mother guaranteed me that we would all have a wonderfully exciting and educational experience that I would never forget. I didn't like it, but my feelings about the matter didn't factor into the inevitable. The van was a totally unexpected sidestep from the manner in which I'd believed we were getting to Australia. At nine years old, I wasn't thrilled at all. I had been excited about the huge jumbo jet we were going to fly in for eighteen hours, not traveling across multiple countries in a small van with my stepdad and older sister in it!

There wasn't anything wrong with Ryan, as far as stepdads go. He was always nice to me when there was reason to communicate, but for the most part he just kept to himself. One time he came in to my bedroom before he went to work and asked me if he could borrow some money out of my piggy bank for some donuts for his breakfast. I had been surprised that he'd asked, but I said he could take the coins anyway. Other than that, contact was limited. I hardly saw him except for every day at dinner and on the weekends. We were not close, like I felt that my father and I had been before he left, but I liked him well enough to feel like he was part of the family. Although Ryan did not actively participate in arranging family outings, he would come with us on the weekends when we would go blackberry picking beside the river, or take long walks around the lovely town of Clifton. He was always game for almost anything in a stoic way. Ryan was a few years younger than Mother, but you couldn't tell that there was an age difference between them by their looks. Anyway, regardless of whether I liked him or not, we were all going to be extremely close for the next few weeks.

My sister, Jane, was funny to me and used to make me laugh relentlessly all the time. Mother would come into our room on a regular basis and tell us to settle down. We had to be at least ten feet away from each other for this to occur. The van had barely six feet of separation space in it. I wasn't quite sure how that would work, seeing as we had a long way to travel. Still, this was the way it was, and Mother encouraged the whole family to endure and enjoy it.

Before long, we were getting immunizations and medications to travel. Smallpox, cholera, malaria, and other diseases were of concern where we were traveling, so we all had to be inoculated. Being administered painful shots was anything but pleasing to me, and I was none too happy about the whole incident. Still, it was what it was, and being protected from disease was part of the travel arrangements. My mother had planned carefully for every detail of the trip. Apart from all the documentation, passports, visas, and horrible vaccines, she worked out every item we would need on our journey, right down to how many bars of soap we would use. Space was an issue, so nothing unnecessary could be packed in the van, which Jane and I had nicknamed the Dinosaur. We called it that because it was green and old, not because of its size!

Mother also worked out all the financial aspects of the trip. Apparently she had been saving for several months for this event, working overtime and cutting back. Conserving those funds was a concern. We needed to have plenty of cash available for the long haul, while putting enough away for when we arrived in Australia. The idea was simple. Once we reached our destination and found a home Down Under, we would have all our other belongings shipped over, and that took money. The actual process was left for my Uncle Seward to take care of once he received word of our progress. The aim was not to spend too much extra on food, clothing, or accommodations while traveling, so we would have plenty left to have the rest of our stuff sent over.

For the trip, we packed enough clothing so that we could change every day and have it all cleaned for the next week. Food consisted of boxed mashed potatoes and canned fruits, vegetables, fish, and meats.

As we were British, of course sugar, dry milk, and tea were top priority. We also brought salt, pepper, and cooking spices so we could add some flavor to our meals. We packed bottles of vitamins, minerals, and glucose tablets as backup nutrients. We would purchase fresh foods such as eggs, bread, and milk in each country as we drove through. Water was the only other item that we would have to obtain. We acquired special cleansing tablets that we could add to the water just in case it wasn't completely safe. The van was equipped with a large fifteen-gallon carboy for water that we could pump into a small stainless-steel sink. Nothing that we would need along the way was left out. Mother organized it all meticulously, to be followed precisely and as methodically as possible as we progressed through the weeks to the desired location, which was a seaport in India. Mother had spent so much time on planning that it could only be considered perfect. If any preparation had been left out, that issue would be addressed at the time; nothing could go wrong. The only exception to the plan was the unlikely event of the unexpected.

Although the adult plans appeared to be going well, one issue that troubled me was that we could not take Katie, our dog, with us. As I was a child, this was a big deal. She had been with us since I was six—that was one third of my whole life, and I felt like we were leaving a member of the family. My mother guaranteed that my uncle would take excellent care of her. Although reluctant to leave Katie behind, I believed that Uncle Seward would take care of her, as plenty of our family members loved the fluffy mutt because she was so cute and well-behaved. She was a black, raggedy-haired Scottish/Cairn terrier mix who had puppy eyes to die for. I felt somewhat reassured knowing that she would be with my uncle and not with a stranger. In the back of my mind, I was hoping that I could ask him to send her to Australia once we were settled in our new home, maybe along with our belongings. That was, however, an issue that I couldn't dwell on, and I had to trust that the best arrangement had been made for her—for now, anyway.

Mother estimated that it would take about four weeks to drive from England to India, where we would embark on a ship, vehicle and all, that would take us as close to Perth as possible. Once in Perth, we would meet up with relatives on my grandmother's side of the family. All but two of eleven children, my grandaunts and granduncles, had emigrated from England to Australia over the years. I knew none of them. My grandmother, whom we called Nan, and my Great-Aunt

Doris were the last of the sibling pack that still lived in England. Nan planned on being in Perth to greet us. Once reunited, we would all start our new lives in Australia, never to look back at foggy old England again. A future of sunshine and beaches for us: it was as straightforward as that.

I felt apprehensive about the entire situation, but for the most part, it changed to enthusiasm as we came closer to setting off on our voyage. I forgot about the imaginary fun we were going to have on the jumbo jet, and I focused more on what Jane and I were going to do all day in the back of the Dinosaur for a month. I gathered up many of my possessions, including ice skates, book collections, and all my toys, to pack in the van. It was way too much, so I had to single out a few of my favorite personal effects from the huge pile of belongings that had accumulated on the living room floor. My mother even picked out two of her beloved plush animals to take along with her; ironically they were koala bears. She instructed us not to bring too many unnecessary items, only a few well-liked toys, a couple of books to read, puzzle and crossword magazines, pens, pencils, drawing paper, and blank journals in which to write down everything we did. Keeping logs of all our encounters was intended to educate and inspire us later in our lives. The intention was for us to look back in our diaries in years to come and marvel over the experience.

Jane and I didn't want to write anything. She was more into music and drawing. She had a unique style that could only be considered abstract art: colorful pen-and-ink renderings that were extremely weird. She packed up some drawing paper and colored felt pens. I guessed she would draw her experiences. At that point in my life, the last thing on my mind was writing. My penmanship was awful, and my spelling was worse. I decided, just in case there was anything of interest to write about, to find something that could be made into a journal. From the dwindling pile of junk, I unearthed a small, red cloth-covered book with blank pages inside. It had a gold lock and an extremely small key. My Aunt Clary had given it to me a long time ago. I figured that it would suffice for recording the so-called adventure, if I had the desire to do so someday. Contrary to her own advice, my mother didn't take anything in which to write down her experiences of the trip. This was mainly because she was the predominant driver and wouldn't have time to sit back and write. The only books she took were our joint passport and a small green notebook covered in flowers that would suffice as the ledger of expenses. Apart from her koalas and clothes, the only other item she took was a pathetically inadequate Instamatic camera that took a tiny film cartridge that held twelve frames. The camera was loaded with one, and we had three extra cartridges. For a trip this extensive bringing two or three cameras and about four hundred rolls of film to accurately record events would have been a great idea, but the Instamatic was the extent of our photographic equipment. As for Ryan, he did not pack anything but his clothes. He was still not completely happy about the whole situation.

The last few days in Bristol were spent rummaging through our belongings, reorganizing the boxes of household items, and repacking our luggage until we had the van articles down to a manageable quantity. We had to reevaluate our estimate of available space numerous times before we finally had it right. The huge book collection I wanted to bring ended up whittled down to about ten books. I took some of my favorite titles: *Rapunzel, The Sword and the Stone, Bennett Cerf's Book of Riddles,* and a few others. I wasn't happy about leaving my extensive collection of children's literature, but there was nothing that could be done.

By the time we separated and boxed up everything that would be shipped to Australia, it was close to the day we were leaving. Mother told me to do one last sweep of the apartment before we finally departed. I ran through all the rooms, confirming that everything was in order and that nothing had been left behind. The bathroom was the last place to check, and everything was pretty well emptied out and clean. I checked the top drawer of the vanity and found a small, unopened box. Inside it were three tiny pink soaps shaped like roses. I called to Mother and told her what I had found. She told me to leave them, as they were more for decoration than for use, and they were so small that no one could possibly make use of them anyway. I stared at the little rose shapes and took a whiff of the flowery scent. I liked them and had to disagree that they had no use. Against Mother's orders, I stuck them in my pocket and made the decision to take them with us. Once all the apartment checks were done, we closed the front door for the last time and proceeded to the van. We hauled our pallet of boxes to Uncle Seward for temporary storage at his house until we were ready to reclaim them later down the road. An emotional send-off took place soon after we dropped off the crates, and then it was time for us to leave. We said our good-byes to Uncle Seward, gave Katie a big doggy hug, and left that day, van stuffed with our remaining possessions. Our first stop was London.

We stayed in London with friends for a couple of days before we started the journey to Australia. Our friends Fiona and Todd were in their fifties. Mother had known them for years. Fiona was Scottish. She was a rotund woman with long, gray hair that she usually kept up in a bun. She looked like the typical grandmother. She loved cooking food—and eating it apparently more. I loved to hear her speak in her Scottish accent. But there was something a wee bit menacing about her that I could never quite figure out. Todd, on the other hand, was quite the opposite. He was from Wales. He was a quiet man with a thin frame and wiry salt-and-pepper hair that always appeared to flop one way or the other, and it was always half greased down. Hair aside, he seemed a kind old soul. I would have liked to listen to his accent once in a while, but he was such a silent man. Together, they reminded me of the nursery rhyme about Jack Sprat.

Arrangements were made to meet up with Fiona and Todd in Iran. We would spend some time in the city of Tehran while visiting a mutual friend called Minah who lived there. Fiona and Todd would fly there two weeks after we left London, and settle in before we arrived by van. It was a means of tracking our progress and of checking that everything had gone to plan, while giving Fiona and Todd an excuse to take a few weeks' vacation in an exotic country while spending time with acquaintances. Knowing that we would meet up with someone we knew along the way also made the whole traveling to strange, new places less foreboding.

After spending two days in London, we set off early one foggy morning in April. Fiona, Todd, and their Pekingese called Angel came downstairs from their Montague Mansions apartment to see us off. Once settled in the van, I looked back through the window to wave good-bye to them, but they had already gone back inside. I didn't blame them, as it was freezing cold that morning. Angel reminded me of Katie. I felt sad again that I was leaving her behind. She was family, but life still went on, and we had an adventure to go on. The sadness turned into a mixture of anxiety and excitement as we began the official first day of our journey.

We had some initial problems with the Dinosaur while trying to start it in the cold, but soon we took off down foggy Baker Street to our first foreign destination, France. After a couple of hours on the road, I started to get bored. I asked my mother on several occasions if we were there yet, and I was advised never to speak those words again, as the trip was going to be at least four weeks long. I sat twiddling my thumbs for a while and then tried to lure Jane away from her drawing. She wasn't interested in interacting with me. It was probably better anyway that we didn't start playing, as we would have ended up being loud, and annoying Mother, which I had already succeeded in doing by asking too many times if we were there yet. I was at the end of my tether with boredom when it occurred to me that this would be a good time to start recording events in my journal. I picked up the red book and fumbled around with the ridiculously miniscule key to open it up. Finally, I opened the lock and began writing down the events that had occurred thus far. My first entry began with the day, month, and year.

Day One: April 8, 1975

We woke up at five past five in the morning; we dressed, had breakfast, and went to the van to start our journey. Jane and I were sitting in the back seat. It was really cold that morning. It had been a frosty night and was really foggy in the morning. Ryan was driving first. He put the key in the ignition and turned, but not much happened except a slight rolling of the motor and a sort of whining noise. All I wanted was for the heater to hurry and warm the vehicle up. Ma and Jane jumped out of the van and started to push. They had pushed it half way down Crawford Street and still the motor did not start. Next Ryan jumped out of the van and started pushing and steering at the same time while turning the ignition. I thought I should help so I clambered out and grabbed the side door and put my all in to it. Finally the motor began to make a putt-putt sound. It started. I knew my muscle power would get the old thing to go although I had thought it to be will power. After the van started we jumped in one by one so we would not be left behind and we finally began the trip to get to Dover.

At first it looked as though we wouldn't get very far, as the van kept on making peculiar noises, but it held up, and we made it to Dover in good time. From this location, we needed to board a vessel to cross over the Strait of Dover, a body of water that separates England from France. But at the port there were delays in the running of ferries, due to the inclement weather. Consequently, there were long queues of cars, trucks, and vans parked about the dock. We didn't make it on our scheduled ferry, so we just sat there waiting with other vehicles until the pace picked up. An hour or so passed while we sat stagnant, watching huge hovercraft float in and out of the harbor. Other vehicles were boarding ferries and departing to their destinations, which irritated me because I wanted to hurry and get on the boat. My mother always used to tell me I had ants in my pants when I was impatient, and this was one of those times. It felt like we were never going to get a ride, but finally it was our turn. We had been waiting for what seemed like an eternity, but now we were moving. My mood changed from frustration to enthusiasm as we proceeded toward the ferry gates.

We had to go through a series of checkpoints and finally show our tickets and passports before we could board. The hour we had spent watching other vehicles coming and going had already piqued my interest. Imagining all those people buzzing back and forth across the English Channel, for who knew what reasons, was intriguing. It was a very thought-provoking sight. Already the trip was proving to be curiously stimulating, mostly because it was unfamiliar. I could hardly contain myself in anticipation of more new experiences.

I had never been on a boat before. I found it thrilling being able to stay in the van while driving onto the ferry. Originally, I'd thought that a crane or some machinery was going to lift the vehicle onto the ferry like cargo, and we would board by foot, but after watching everyone else drive on, I knew what to expect. It looked as if it would be entertaining, like an amusement park ride or something of that nature. I had fired up my adrenaline imagining that as soon as we tried to drive onto the ferry, we would fall through a crack between land and boat and go crashing into the freezing cold water. I was confident that we really wouldn't, but it must have been an unconscious fear for me to even think of such a bizarre notion. After successfully boarding the ferry, we had to leave the vehicle area and go on deck until we arrived at our destination, which was Calais.

My mother had told me that she never did very well on boats, and before we even took off, she was getting a bit queasy with the slight rocking of the docked ferry. She took a couple of seasickness pills and told Jane and me to go amuse ourselves and look around. Ryan stayed with her to make sure she would be okay, so Jane and I took off like a couple of curious kittens. I didn't know that a ferry was so big inside. It had several floors with a cafeteria, bathrooms, and even slot machines. Jane and I played around with those for a short while before we realized we didn't have the correct change to play. We had a big bag of pennies, but the game took a five-pence piece per pull. Shortly after the letdown of the slot machines, I felt movement. We ran up on deck to watch as we left the dock. Mother and Ryan were already standing by the railing, looking out toward land. I ran up beside them and watched as the seawater splashed up the back and the sides of the ferry in huge, white waves that looked like soapsuds. The wind brought up cold water that sprayed in our faces like a fine rain, except it was salty and gross and smelled like fish. I added that to my ever-growing mental list of new experiences. As we moved farther and farther away from the coastline through the fine mist and fog, I could see the white cliffs of Dover. It reminded me of the song, but without the bluebirds. I was already awed by the adventure so far, and we had barely left British waters. After we went back inside, I wrote down the events in my journal. Apparently, writing was going to be constructive after all.

Chapter 2

France

About two hours after we left Dover, we were docking in Calais. All driving passengers were called back to their respective vehicles. Once everyone settled in, we drove single file through a checkpoint, where we attained our first passport stamp. When we'd first received the passport, Mother had showed me the empty spaces where each country would leave its mark. I imagined colorful images that would cover the entire page and represent some artistic expression of the nation. I was actually upset that I did not get a passport all to myself. Instead Jane and I were listed in Mother's passport as "accompanied by." Being minor children I guess it was easier to get the family deal. Ryan had his own passport, but I was not interested in that one, only the one which my name was in. Anyway I asked if I could be the keeper of the passport. It was like a scrapbook of countries visited, tangible evidence that we were making headway. Naturally, the answer was no, but my mother did say she would let me see each stamp as we passed through the borders. I couldn't wait to see the first image in the passport, so when I finally spied the impression, there was an anticlimactic moment as I stared at the simple ink marking. As plain as it was to the eye, the stamp represented a sign of progress, so it suddenly became something spectacular. Soon after the viewing, the thin black book was closed and placed back in its very special place in a travel bag that never left Mother's side.

France was the first foreign country I had ever visited, so I had no idea what to expect. Mother explained to me that all people were basically the same except for their languages. I was relieved to hear that, and I had a better idea of how the trip would progress. If language was the only difference, then it would be as straightforward as going on a day trip back in England, except for a longer distance. I felt that I could deal with that.

Once we were firmly on French soil, we started toward Paris. The goal from there was a small town called Dijon. The first noticeable difference was that we were driving on the wrong side of the road. Mother quickly corrected my assumption by telling me that there was no right or wrong; it was just a matter of what side each country decided to drive on. She also mentioned that the only countries that drove on the left were British based, and that most of the world drove on the right. It dawned on me then that the British were the ones driving on the wrong side. I wanted to have a long discussion on the how's and whys of choosing the correct side, but Mother cut me off by telling me not to ponder the small things in life, and just to enjoy France as it was.

The drive down to Paris from Calais was simple and straightforward. We saw the same basic landscape as in England: green fields, farms, horses, cows, sheep, and such. Nothing really stood out as impressive enough to write about, as it was pretty much like the countryside back home. But as we neared the Paris roads, the view started changing. The streets quickly became full of vehicles that were driving insanely fast. We came to a large roundabout where everyone was honking and hooting and driving like a maniac in a high-speed, uniform flow. It was madness like nothing I had seen before. If a driver was not quick enough to make it into one of these fast-paced lanes, the other drivers slammed on their horns, which explained the insane noise. It was a good thing that my mother had excellent driving skills, because we drove out of that predicament pretty quickly, which made me feel more comfortable, as I had imagined we would be going around and around for hours, stuck in a never-ending circle. It made me dizzy thinking about it; I actually felt physically sick. The chaos came about rapidly, but fortunately it ended just as fast, and soon we were driving in a normal fashion along a quaint Paris road.

As a brief side trip, we went to view the Eiffel Tower. We didn't stop or get out and use one of our twelve photo frames to snap the tower. We simply drove around the closest streets to get a glimpse. It was a straightforward drive-by viewing. My mother told us a few facts about the tower, like how it was called Eiffel after the man who designed it, how it was at least nine hundred and fifty feet tall, and that there was an elevator that could take you to the top where you could view the entirety of Paris. I thought it to be an incredible piece of art, basically because of its size, and wished we could have had more time to look at it. But we all knew that this was a mini excursion from the practical and not a vacation.

Once we passed through the city, the streets began to clear again. We had some trouble actually getting away from there, as all roads appeared to lead back to Paris, but eventually the correct route was found, and we managed to break free from the clutches of the deceiving signposts. We made incredibly good time, probably in the rush to get away from the madness of the bustling capital. My mother was adamant that we follow her schedule. The success of the trip depended on arriving at the desired locations on time, as planned. That afternoon, we arrived in Fontainebleau, a town about fifty miles from Paris. We drove into the parking lot at the Hôtel de Londre, right across from the sixteenth-century Royal Château, also known as the Palace of Fontainebleau. We were going to stay at the Hôtel de Londre that night.

The plan for nights was simple. We would camp every few days and then rent a hotel room to take showers, get a good night's sleep, and reorganize the van. This was going to be our first hotel stay of the trip. Mother went on ahead to check into our reserved rooms, while Jane and I stayed with Ryan in the van and gathered up a few belongings that we would take in with us. Evidently, the receptionist said that there were no reservations in our name, and the only room available was an enormously high-priced suite. There was no way that my mother was going to be swindled into paying a penny more that what they had quoted for our reservation. Noticeably perturbed, she stormed out to the van and told us we needed to find a place to park for the night, as we would not be staying there after all. Everyone sat quietly as we waited for her to decide what to do. She drove five feet away, off the hotel property, and shut down the van. We camped in the Dinosaur that night with a marvelous front-seat view of the brightly lit-up Palace of Fontainebleau. It wasn't quite the luxurious comfort of the hotel that we had been expecting, but it worked. We were all tired and needed to rest after the first hectic day of our four-week journey.

Early the next morning, we went into the hotel's café and ate a continental breakfast. It was different from the usual cereal and milk or traditional British breakfast of sausage, eggs, and bacon. It consisted of a roll, toast, and jam. I thought it to be more of an appetizer, but I didn't complain, because that was how breakfast was done here in France. Mother told me a saying that related to adjusting to new places. "When in Rome, do as the Romans do!" she said with a matter-of-fact nod.

I knew that there had to be merit to the saying, and I took it seriously, pondering the implications of every word. I understood the basic point she was making, except as far as I remembered we were not going to Rome.

Before starting back on the road, we made a quick stop to view the famous architecture of the Palace of Fontainebleau. It was considered a structure of beauty, a wonder of French history. It looked pretty at night when the lights were shining on it, but in the day, it just looked like a big old building to me, and I was told nobody lived there, so it seemed like a waste of space. Shortly after staring aimlessly at the massive, ineffectual structure, we loaded into the Dinosaur and were back on the road. I decided to write more about what we had done so far.

Day Two: April 9, 1975

We woke up at six thirty in the morning. It was freezing when we woke up. We were pulling blankets off each other all night, I tried to take Jane's blanket, but I ended up with one. We dressed in as warm as clothes as we could find, ate breakfast in a café at the Hotel De Londre, and started the next part of our trip. Yesterday we were in Paris, we saw the Eiffel Tower. This morning we had a look at a palace with a gray or green roof across the street from the hotel.

By now, we were beginning to see a few places that were different from England. The adventure of being in France set in, and we started to enjoy the day. We stopped for lunch near a river. It was somewhat cold, but after being cramped up in the van for a few hours, we enjoyed being able to get out and stretch our legs. Jane and I were encouraged to run about and get some exercise, probably in an attempt to wear us out so we wouldn't have the energy to squabble with each other, as we did so often for fun. I ran to a nearby field to pet some lambs, but they just frolicked off to their mothers. I then decided I would play catch with Jane. For some odd reason, one of the favorite toys I chose to take with me was a small plastic ball with animals printed on it, which obviously meant something to me, as I also drew a picture of it in my journal. Jane was not really thrilled by throwing a ball around, but she did so to appease me. I didn't remember bringing that ball back to the van after that particular day. Perhaps I thought it had fallen in the river, or that I had lost it, and that was why I drew a picture of it.

After a relaxing lunch, we all clambered back into the van, and once again, off we went. Jane and I started to play various games with one of our several decks of cards. No matter what we played, Jane always beat me. I had to deal with her devilish giggles every time I lost a game. Other than my inevitable losing streak at rummy, everything else appeared to be running smoothly until the van started to make some weird noises. The weather started to get really cold, and to make matters worse, there were signs of snow. Two hours after our leisurely lunch by the river, the van broke down. We were about twenty miles from Dijon. Either my mother found a way to call for help, or luck was on our side, because within about five minutes, a tow truck was there to take us to the nearest garage. The cold weather and signs of snow were now a full-fledged blizzard with the biggest snow chunks in history slamming at high speed sideways on our front window. Thirty minutes later, we were driven up to a small building that looked like a mechanic's garage. Unfortunately, it was late, and the garage was not open. We were dropped off right there, and we had to wait until the next day to get the van looked at. As soon as the gentleman who towed us was paid, he vanished into the winter storm. Ryan and my mother told Jane and me to wait inside the van while they looked around for a place to stay.

About fifteen minutes later, they returned, soaking wet. The umbrella that they were using had four inches of snow on it and was buckling under the weight. It draped around both of them like a sad igloo. If the situation had not been quite so dire, it would have been kind of funny. On their walk, they had found a small police station and asked for assistance, but apparently the police could not help. In fact, my mother said no one there spoke English. This place had no motel, hotel, or Holiday Inn. The only enclosed area that was visible through the thick snow was a bus station. We all scampered over to the lit building. Technically, no one was allowed to be in the station at night, but some kind soul felt sorry for us and let us stay in the enclosed area of the extremely small terminal. It is no wonder he felt bad for us, as we were all freezing and must have looked pitiful. As kind as he was to let us stay, there was a downside. There were no seats or benches of any kind, and the floor was made of vinyl tiles. We had to sleep on the hard surface of those tiles. It was quite uncomfortable and miserably cold, but it was inside, and inside was better than being outside in the snow. I had thought the night before when we had slept in the van was unpleasant, but this was much worse. I was really beginning to despise the cold, and I couldn't wait to be basking on the beaches of Australia.

Day Three: April 10, 1975

We woke up at four in the morning. We slept in a coach station. We were cold, so cold, so freezing cold that we nearly turned to ice. We could not understand the Frenchman that let us stay, but it was time for us to leave. In broken English and French, the man spoke to us. Jane said the man suggests we eat snails, they are really good.

Did I mention that not one of us spoke any language except English? Jane spoke some French that she'd learned at school, but she was nowhere near fluent enough to communicate effectively. With the help of charades, the Frenchman had let us know we could stay in the terminal, but by four in the morning, we were told that it was time to vacate. The first coaches were going to arrive, and we could not be seen sleeping there when the passengers arrived. We thanked the generous man and walked back to the Dinosaur. It was still snowing heavily. Still tired, we wrapped ourselves up as best we could and stayed in the van for a few hours, until the garage mechanic arrived to open for business.

Later that morning, a knock on the window woke us. The windows were all steamed up, and we had to wipe away a hole in the condensation so we could see outside. There stood the mechanic. Mother and Ryan opened up the side and went around the back of the van to open the hatch to the motor. The mechanic checked the engine and told us that it had seized up completely. We would need a new motor, or at least an overhauled one, for the van to ever run again. This was obviously upsetting news, and Ryan was already contemplating our return to England, but my mother was determined to continue. We knew better than to question a decision that Mother made, as she often took alternate suggestions as insults to her intelligence. She would mistakenly look at it as a poke at her personality and get all upset. Nothing could change her mind once she had decided to accomplish something, so a large chunk of our travel money went to purchase a new motor. This process was going to take at least two or three days, maybe longer, before the van would be ready to drive again.

While the van was being repaired, we went on to Dijon, which happened to be less than a quarter of a mile away. It was a quaint little village with cobblestone roads and small shops. I learned that this was the town that the famous Dijon mustard came from. The farmlands here were filled with snow, so I couldn't tell if there were any mustard plants growing in the fields. Still, it reminded me of a day trip the previous summer when we drove Sunny to the small town of Cheddar in England. I was told that it was where the original cheddar cheese was made. Cheddar was located smack in the middle of dairy farmland. I knew this on account of all the black-and-white cows we saw on the way down there, and so it seemed feasible. It was all starting to make sense. I had never really thought about the origins of food, or anything much else, for that matter. So it was somewhat interesting to learn that mustard was made from a plant and did not just spontaneously appear in a jar. Anyhow, here we were walking around and trying to find lodgings in the freezing cold streets of Dijon. Eventually we found the loveliest hotel on the face of the earth! They had food, the best coffee ever, and warm beds.

Day Three, April 10, 1975

We made it to Dijon. It was not so far away from the coach station. Jane and I don't want to eat snails. We looked for a hotel and found one. We drank really good coffee, such good coffee, we drank and drank and almost turned to coffee. Not a lot happened today, but we had a really big sandwich to eat, it was so good, but I could not eat it all. We went to our rooms and took showers and washed our hair really well. We took a nice nap. After, we went downstairs to have more food. Now it is bedtime and we are going to sleep.

There was not much we could do while we were waiting for the van to get fixed. We spent most of our time enjoying the exquisite coffee from the hotel and eating the delicious sandwiches. Mother was constantly looking through her ledger, reinventing the way we would spend the remaining cash. She was also anxious to keep up with the schedule she had so carefully devised. At this rate, we would be a few days behind, and that was not good. Finally, she came to the conclusion that we were going to be fine. The ledger slammed shut, and she had a satisfied look on her face. The next morning, we went on a shopping spree. An entry in my journal for that day was as follows:

Day Four, April 11, 1975

The beds last night were so warm. Jane and I slept on a mattress that made us fall into each other. It had fifty blankets on it! It was so warm. We want to stay there forever! The bathroom was funny. It had a toilet, and then another strange toilet next to it. I am going to use the English toilet. Today we went shopping. Ma bought me pants and a nice warm scarf at the market. Jane bought three pairs of socks, red, blue, and yellow. In the market I saw a man cutting up big fish into pieces and selling them to

people. On the way back to the hotel, Jane and I saw a cute puppy
in the pet store. It was a Chihuahua. It looked nothing like Katie,
but it reminded me of her. We asked Ma if we could buy it. She
said no, it would be too expensive. Jane and I went back to see
how much the puppy cost. It was a lot of Francs; we could not
afford to buy it. When we came back to the hotel we wrote
postcards to Nan.

After our outing to the market and the misguided attempts to
acquire a new pet, I started writing to my grandmother. I was using the
only pen available in the hotel room. Jane wanted to write a card too,
but I told her that she must wait for me to finish first or go and find
another pen. I took my time as I carefully wrote a few words to Nan.
Jane was getting impatient with me for taking so long, and she started
pulling the socks off my feet. It was a stupid game that we played back
in England when I actually had the space to try to get her socks off.
The game was stupid because I never won. This time it was even
dumber, as I was doing something important. Plus it was cold, and
I didn't want to have my socks taken off. Finally, I gave up and ended
my postcard. Jane took the pen and card from me and read it.

Dear Nanny,

I hope you are feeling well. We saw a really tiny puppy in a shop.
It was seventy-five pounds. Ma did not buy it. We don't know
why. Hee hee. See you soon.

Love, Jennifer.

After Jane read it, she took the pen and added "and Jane" at the
bottom of the postcard. I gathered she had lost interest in writing her
own by the time I had finished.

By the twelfth of April, we were ready to go again. The van was
brought to us, and we checked out of the hotel. We went shopping for
the last items we would need, such as six loaves of delicious French
bread, like the sandwiches were made from back at the hotel. We also
picked up fresh milk and eggs that we would fry up for breakfast the
next day. Before long, we were on the road, trying to speed our way to
the next country. The plan was to drive to Switzerland and through the
Alps to Austria. We would then continue on to Hungary, Russia, and
then south to Iran, where we would meet up with Fiona and Todd and

stay with Minah. This was an event that I could hardly wait for. But it was early days, and we were still in wintery old France.

Without a doubt, it would have been an excellent idea to purchase tire chains for the van, because it snowed constantly from the time we ate lunch by the river. The snow had started off as faint sleet and within hours turned into an all-out snowstorm, and it was still going strong. The roads had a hazardous layer of snow-covered ice, which made them dangerous to drive on. Since the trip had already been postponed for three days, driving onward was a risk we had to take. From Dijon, we drove southeast toward Mont Blanc in the Swiss Alps. We would be taking the mountain route from France that would land us in the next country, Switzerland. Several roads led to Mont Blanc, and that initially caused some driver-to-navigator disagreements, which happened quite often. We turned around and went different ways several times, but eventually we ended up back on track. Apart from the navigation issues, there were other concerns regarding the snow situation. We heard rumors that there were avalanches up on some parts of the mountains that made them inaccessible. I was unaware of what exactly an avalanche was, but I did know they had something to do with the snow and that they were dangerous. Trying to figure out which was the safest way to go was causing problems. We eventually reached a mountain pass and started an upward route toward the Mont Blanc area. We had not driven very far when we came to a roadblock. People stood outside their vehicles, talking to each other, more than likely about the road conditions due to the snow. They told us that we couldn't go past the roadblock and that we should try another location farther south. That was somewhat frustrating, but we turned around and drove another thirty minutes or so until we reached an alternative route to get through the Alps.

On the way up, there were the same concerns with drivers turning back down the snowy roads to find different routes. We stopped the van and tried to locate someone who spoke English. The only English-speaking person we could find was an Austrian who said it was extremely dangerous to go the way we wanted, because a small avalanche made the road perilous; but he also said there was no law stopping us, so we could always try, and maybe we would make it. There were no official warnings stating that passage through the mountain was illegal, so with even a minute chance that we could take that road and get through to Switzerland, we tried. We drove in the direction of the terrifying avalanche. I heard the Austrian say that the avalanche was small, so I wondered if there was really a threat at all. Mother was raring to go, but we had to take it easy. We slowly drove by several people shaking their heads in disbelief that we would risk the snowy pass.

As we drove away from the small crowd, the area seemed to turn completely white. There was an eerie feeling as we trundled forward. The Dinosaur crept up the steep mountain, in a manner not only designed to deter us from sliding back down but also to prevent the stirring of avalanches. I knew for a fact that I didn't want to see one. It was late in the evening, but the snow somehow lit up the surroundings. There was a strange, peaceful feeling as we drove silently over the heavily laid virgin snow. Every now and again, we slid back a few feet, despite the extremely careful driving. My mother controlled the vehicle with expertise, but even with all the cautious steering and moving of the van, it took a sideways glide down the slick, snow-covered road. When we stopped, we were diagonally positioned across both lanes. We were not in any immediate danger of getting into a collision with another car, as no one else was quite as enthusiastic about traveling up that path as Mother was, but there was the chance that we could slide off the side of the road and down the steep, tree-covered embankment, which would have us impaled on gnarly branches and ragged-edged rocks. By then, my mother had started to feel uneasy, and she changed her mind about going up that way. The van was stuck in a precarious position. Every time Mother tried to drive it forward or back, we just slid more, toward the tops of trees. We decided it would probably be safer to move the vehicle ourselves, so we all jumped out and began pushing the van to face back down the mountain.

After about ten minutes of huffing and puffing and slipping all over the place to get the Dinosaur back on track, we just stood there and stared at each other. There were no words to be said. Mother had a look on her face that I was not familiar with. It looked like it could be a cross between frustration and defeat, but she was not saying anything. Breaking the silence, Jane threw a snowball in my direction. With that, Ryan picked up some snow and started throwing it in the general direction of Mother. At first she was displeased, but soon she laughed. With that, we all just started throwing snowballs and began having a complete group mental breakdown, laughing so hard that tears came to our eyes. Plus it was probably about negative three Fahrenheit outside, which also has the tendency to bring tears to one's eyes. In an effort to keep this a memorable moment, my mother took out her Instamatic and took a few pictures of us bounding about in the snow. We didn't stay outside too long, which was probably a good idea, as we did not intend to die of hypothermia or, worse, be killed by an avalanche. After all, we had been causing a commotion.

Day Five, April 12, 1975

Today we were going to Switzerland. We drove up a lot of different mountains, but could not get through. There are avalanches that could kill people. We drove up this one mountain, but Ma said she felt sick going up, so we turned around. Now we are going to Italy.

We needed to come up with a different plan. While up on the mountain, we made some hot cocoa to warm ourselves up. There was a considerable amount of driving to undertake if we were to get back down to the foothill and find someplace else where we could drive across the Alps. Mother and Ryan went back and forth trying to devise a different strategy. Eventually, they just decided to go back and see what other folk were doing. On our way down, we ran into some people who were in the same predicament, which was not a surprise, considering the Alpine passes were the most direct and busy routes from France to Switzerland. Many of those people would have to divert. The people we spoke to said that they would probably go south and get a carrier train that passed through the mountains and came out at the other end in Italy. They said that the next train was scheduled for nine that evening. Decisions, decisions—what were we going to do? We could wait a few more days to see if the weather changed and the roads cleared, but that would cause even more delays, or we could follow in the other people's footsteps, or rather tire tracks, and take an alternate route to Italy. The reality was that we were not getting to Switzerland through the mountains that day. With map in hand and a few quick calculations, my mother was driving with enthusiasm toward Chamonix, to catch the nine o'clock train to Italy.

Despite the thick snow, we made excellent time, and before long we were driving onto a train. I thought that driving onto the ferry back in Dover had been fun, but this was super cool. We had to stay at the station for a few hours while everyone traveling with a vehicle on that train was checked for anything illegal. I wasn't sure what items were illegal, but I didn't worry, because I knew that whatever they were, we didn't have any. When our turn to be searched finally arrived, the customs officer who checked our vehicle was extremely paranoid. First, he checked our huge, green Tupperware bowl full of white sugar. In French, he asked my mother what it was. She opened it up and put some on her tongue, showing him that it was a food item. He took a sniff and then decided it was acceptable. He lifted up one of the back seats, which were also storage space where we kept much of our canned and dry food. The inspector noticed my mother's rather extensive collection of exotic Indian spices. He motioned for her to show him what they were. My mother reached in and grabbed one of the tins that was already opened for use and told him it was curry powder. Because he was having trouble understanding what it was, she put some of the ground spice on her tongue to show him that it was also for eating. She took a whiff of the brown powder and offered the tin to him so he could sample the divine aroma. He was getting rather agitated by now and definitely didn't want to sample the spice in any form. So finally Mother found a container that was factory sealed, showing him that it was a store-bought Indian cooking product. While he was looking at the label with a confused and rather suspicious look on his face, my mother blurted out words that widened my eyes with disbelief.

"Do you know? You look like Steve McQueen!" she said in her proper English accent with a look of complete sincerity on her face.

"Steve McQueen?" the confused man said in his French accent.

"Yes, you know—very good-looking film star!" she continued as she pointed to his face and made circular motions with her finger.

She began naming off several Steve McQueen films. A nod of insight and a stretched-out grin from the man indicated that he understood what she was saying.

"Oui! Steve McQueen, I know eem," he said very happily. "And I look like eem?" he asked while nodding his head in affirmation of his resemblance to the actor.

With that, he put down the spice, checked the tickets and passports, had a quick chat with my mother, and left our vehicle with the hugest Cheshire cat smirk, pasted on his Steve McQueen face that anyone had ever seen. I was completely in shock. I had watched a movie with Steve McQueen in it before we left England, and there was no similarity to him as far as I could see, except maybe for his blue eyes. Still, this apparently pleased him. He gave us the go-ahead, and that was all we needed to press forward on what already seemed like an endless trip by day five. It was odd, because that Frenchman did not speak a word of English until my mother mentioned his so-called likeness to Steve McQueen. Once he had received the alleged compliment, he became rather forthcoming, explaining in a calm and pleasant manner in English that it was his job to be suspicious of everything, and that he had to check our cargo just in case.

I was still trying to fathom the unforeseen action and his reaction to my mother's words, and although it seemed a bit off the wall, I was glad she had pursued an alternate method of approval, because there were still three storage seats left in the back that were unopened and full of food that he might not have recognized. We would have been there all night had he gone through all of our spices and provisions. Still, I was prone to what-if moments, and it occurred to me that being told you look like someone might not always provoke a positive response. What if he did not want to look like Steve McQueen? But he did, and that was the important part. If he had not been satisfied with our cooking practices, we might not have made it on that train ride, and we would have suffered yet another delay. I was surprised at Mother's unexpected act but impressed by her quick thinking and intuitive perception of the fellow. Fortunately, luck was on our side. I asked my mother how she knew that the gentleman would understand what she was saying. She told me that all French people knew how to speak English, but most chose not to. About thirty minutes later, the train's wheels made an angry screeching noise as the train pulled away from the station. Au revoir, France!

Chapter 3

Italy

Jane and I were excited to be in our van on a moving train. We could hardly wait to see the mountains and watch out the window as we entered the long, dark tunnels to bypass all of the inaccessible roads. At first I was hoping we might see an avalanche, which Jane informed me was a large area of snow and ice falling from a higher elevation and not an abominable snowman or anything like that. Even though there were no monsters out there after all, I thought the sight of falling snow would be amazing to witness, until Jane told me that we might get covered in it and die a horrible, freezing-cold death; hence the danger from an avalanche. After hearing that, I kind of hoped we wouldn't see one after all.

I was not the brightest snowflake in the blizzard at nine years old, but I was already beginning to acquire an education at the speed that a snowflake fell in France this time of year. When my mother had told us that we would have a learning experience, she wasn't joking. It was not that I had learned a great deal in these early days of our trip, but my mind had definitely broadened to the great many possibilities that the world possessed. Never before had I thought about anything in particular except what was right in front of me at the time. Now my imagination was at full throttle. I began thinking about all the fascinating elements and potential dangers we might encounter on the train trip ahead of us. The carrier was now in constant motion on its journey through the treacherous and snow-covered mountains, which distracted me out of my daydreaming state. We started off outside with the falling snow and before long were passing under the mountains in pitch black. The train trundled on through the darkness, making a soft, rhythmic sound like someone was tapping gently on drums.

Day Five, April 12, 1975

Jane and I fell asleep. We missed the whole mountain trip. Ma said she saw a smoking volcano, but we did not see anything. I did not even see the man give us our stamp! (I drew a picture of mountains and a volcano.) It is late. We are camping tonight. Ryan made up the beds. We are going back to sleep.

The first thing I wanted to do was to look at our new Italian stamp. My mother insisted it was nothing much to look at, but I still wanted to see it, so she broke down and showed it to me. I looked at the ink stamp with its date and strange foreign words and was mesmerized. It really was not much to look at, much like the French stamp, but it still represented something special: one step closer to our goal. I imagined myself learning how to surf in the clear, blue waters of Australia. I handed the passport back to my mother with a very satisfied feeling of accomplishment, like I had done this thing by myself.

By the time we arrived at the next camp, Jane and I couldn't wait to get out of the confinement of the van and stretch our legs. We had advanced about two hundred miles since our last stop, which had been brief. My mother and Ryan had been taking turns driving, but sitting for long hours, driving or not, can make one quite stiff in the joints. As a passenger on a long driving trip, there is only so much one can do before boredom sets in. Opening the side door for Jane and me to get out was probably like releasing a couple of caged animals after being cooped up for so long. Being upright and able to run around never felt so good.

Jane and I tried to stay focused and occupied while on the road. We made up games, like counting how many red cars we saw in two minutes, or the first one to see a horse could breathe again. I always got blue in the face before I had to give up, leaving Jane as the reigning All Games Champion. Occasionally, Ryan or my mother volunteered to judge the games, but generally Jane was the referee and judge of the final scores. Eventually, when those games became boring, I kept an eye out the window for an amazing sight. Retaining every detail of what I saw was part of my scheme to make the writing in my journal more interesting. Miles went by with nothing different on the horizon. Once in a while, I spotted unfamiliar-shaped structures—a triangular house, a football-shaped building, or a brightly painted barn that sparked my interest. Before I could write the first word, the subject of interest would be way behind us. It was quite disappointing at times, as I really wanted my record of events to be full of interesting and exciting topics. Nonetheless, I had been filling the pages of my journal with this and that, and I knew that whatever I did not write down at the time could be written at a later date, as memory served as the best record for everything that was happening.

During the weeks before we left England, I had expressed my concerns to my mother about school and what I would do without teachers and the classroom. Somewhere along the way she had become an empiricist stating that all I needed to know was right there in front of me. That my experiences would be my teacher. When I argued the point she then told me that only two things were important when it came to learning: having a good memory and being able to read. She always told me that if I could read and remember what I read, I could learn anything. I took that seriously and tried to read as much as I could. The only problem was that we did not have that much of a reading selection while en route, but I figured the same applied to my writing. If I could remember it, I could write it. I was still hoping, though, that we could stop off somewhere interesting and stick around for a while, so I could get a firsthand account of something incredible to jot down, but we never stopped off anywhere for that long. I was quite intrigued with the fact that we had gone to Italy instead of Switzerland and was curious about what we would find there.

From Turin, the other side of the train trip, we had passed through Milan. The cities of Italy were showing signs of being distinctly different from those in France. The center of one town had a huge cathedral and Roman-style buildings that caught my eye. I was going to write a remark about seeing a beautiful cathedral where Catholics prayed, but I thought it redundant, as it should have been obvious, as it was a cathedral. Many times when I would get an idea to record something in my journal, I changed my mind because I didn't want to add an entry unless it was distinctively different or directly applied to an experience.

Apart from the unfortunate occurrence of the van breaking down in France and our stay at the hotel, the majority of the trip so far had been visual. It was mostly see and no do. It was still effectively stimulating, as I had not seen Europe before. As we passed through the towns and cities, I noticed how they differed in style. At first I was not interested in buildings, but as the majority of the trip consisted of passing different places, and the most prominent features were the structures, I had started taking notice of the types of architecture in all the cities we visited. The farther away from England we traveled, the more they changed. I could not help but become curious about them. I asked my mother more and more questions about the individual locations, and the details that I found interesting, but she knew only so much about each country and was definitely not a historian or an architect. The constant questioning must have been similar to that of a three-year-old who has learned the concept of the word "why." Eventually, she asked me not to distract her with too many questions and said to just keep writing everything in my journal. So I continued writing as best I could. I wanted my entries to be more about my experiences and not so much my observations of the surroundings, it was disappointing, but what could I do? Mother was in control, and so I could only write what I saw was happening at the time. I would have liked to be more involved with the decisions, but as a child, naturally I did what I was told. I thought back to the Eiffel Tower and how I would have liked to step into the elevator and go to the top, so I could look over the city of Paris and tremble at the knees with the fear of being way above the ground, but it was one of those things over which I had no control. I don't know how many times Mother reminded us that it was a journey from A to B and not a vacation. It was becoming quite clear already that this was no holiday. All I could do was wait eagerly to reach the next step and hope everything went smoothly so we could hurry up and reach Australia.

Mother had a long list of towns in each country that we would pass through; it was like a written version of steppingstones to get us to where we were going. Already several of them had lines across them, and new names were written in their places as our journey took different turns. Originally, when the plans to go to Switzerland were changed to pass through Italy, Mother said we were going to spend a little more time in some of the Italian towns and actually venture more than twenty feet away from the van. We were to go on a leisurely shopping spree at a market, to restock our fresh food items and pick up postcards with cheerful Italian scenery to send to family and friends. But because of the long detour, it was decided that we should keep on moving after all. We passed the immense city of Milan, with all its giant Gothic buildings and huge cathedrals that looked like they would be fun to examine, but Mother said it was far too crowded a place to stop. She felt uncomfortable, so we drove on to the next town on the list, which was about thirty miles away from Milan.

When we reached the hilly town of Bergamo, we parked for a break. Instead of entering the pretty city that was decorated colorfully with an array of tan houses with red roofs, and towers with massive green domes that reached to the sky from the highest parts of the hills, we stopped on a road just outside town. There were no picnic tables or bathroom facilities. We ate sandwiches and drank tea from the van, and afterward I was forced to urinate behind a bush. I felt awkward, as I knew that someone on the other side might spot me, but at times like this, what is one to do?

Once our quick afternoon tea break was over, we hurried on to the next town. We drove along a route that took us to Verona, another town on the steppingstone list. It was another beautiful city with rectangular white buildings and tall, skinny trees set in between them. If it had been up to me, I would have walked around the streets and ventured into one of the houses to view the magnificent river that ran through the city, but it wasn't. All I could do was view the sights and hope that I never lost the memories of the many different wonderful places I saw. In between Bergamo and Verona, there was a huge lake and several small rivers. It was so inviting to look at that I wanted to stop off and take a swim. I was told that the water was probably too cold to swim in, and that we didn't have time to find out. I was also reminded that once we were in Australia, we could swim every day. I loved the idea of swimming in the ocean and had a spark of new energy. I was encouraged to read a small Australian travel guide that reviewed cities across the great land. I didn't want to read all of that small print, but I didn't mind looking at the pictures. I opened up the book to the middle spread, which had the most wonderful centerfold. It was an Australian reef. The water was pristine and clear. There were beautiful corals and an assortment of colorful fish dotted around the vastness of the rocks. Slap bang in the middle of the reef was a massive, open-mouthed shark with ugly gums and thousands of tiny, sharp teeth that appeared to be facing the cameraman who took the picture. Quickly I slammed the guide closed and went back to viewing the Italian scenery out of the van window. After a few minutes, I took out my journal and began writing about the sights I had seen in Italy.

The next destination was the country of Yugoslavia. In bold letters on our steppingstone list were the countries we needed to pass, and then in smaller print were the cities, towns, and villages that we would travel to. Mother would let Jane and me keep the list, so we knew where we would be going next. It was fun looking at the names and then finding them on our maps. It gave Jane and me something else to do while we were on the road. Because of the detour, my mother had made an alternative route for us to get to Iran. So far, very little of the planned scenario had actually played out, and the organized list of towns and countries looked more like a page of tic-tac-toe than a plan. Still, we were moving on, and that was what counted.

From the big lake near Verona, we drove through Vincenza, and then Padova, and on to Trieste. Crossing off two more towns meant we were progressing on our journey. I was hoping we would be able to stay in Padova and sightsee, but we still had to make up for lost time, so driving on was the only focus. Even though we didn't do any tourist-type exploration in Italy, I could not miss the beauty and elegance of the country. The cities and towns were always pristine and well maintained. They looked like fairy-tale towns.

Our trip through Italy went comparatively smooth. We had no delays or misunderstandings with the locals until we arrived at a little convenience store where we were going to stock up on snacks for the trip. Since we were only in Italy for a short time, my mother had not completely familiarized herself with the insane difference between pounds and lira. After we pumped gas and put all our goodies together, my mother paid for them. She handed the cashier the money and was standing around waiting for her change. The cashier refused to give her money, but as a goodwill gesture, he handed her a chocolate bar. This infuriated my mother, as she couldn't understand why she was not given her change. She tried to get Ryan to take charge, but he did not speak Italian, and he could do no more than any of us; plus he was still talking about heading back to England, as the trip had thus far not been extremely pleasant for him. It was fortunate for us that there was an English-speaking local man who came over just at the right time to explain to my mother that the small amount of change was probably close to half a penny in English money. Blushing, she apologized to the cashier, and we all rushed to the van as quickly as we could and proceeded on our merry way, candy bar in hand!

Italy was an astonishing country as far as the landscape and the towns, but it was still rather disappointing viewing it from a moving vehicle, and other than mentioning every field, mountain, and lake we passed, there was not much to write about in my journal. But in an effort to fill my pages, I always tried to write something.

Day Six, April 13, 1975

In the morning we woke up, packed up our beds, had breakfast, and set off again. We saw more mountains, but did not drive in them. We drove quite far next to a huge river. We stopped for lunch near a lake. We saw unusual birds. I threw them some bread crumbs. We saw a lot of lakes and more rivers. After we drove quite a bit, we saw tiny houses and cottages. We have driven for two hours and twenty minutes. We stopped in a town and went shopping for sweets, and crisps. We have started to drive under big bridges and into long tunnels. It has started to get warmer. Every time we stop off at a camp or a rest stop, people stare at us. The area has a lot of trees and fields. The mountains disperse. I wanted some crisps, but Ma said not now. Jane and I were making faces at each other. She told me I was ugly, so I told Jane she had spots, that she is a spotty face boy. Then I told her I was only joking. Ma keeps looking at the map for something.

We drove through Italy at lightning speed, and before long, we were in Trieste. Mother drove us down through the town so we could observe the environment; she told us to take in as much in as we could of Italy, because soon we would be leaving there for good. My senses were heightened as I tried to take in details of every person, house, and shop we passed. It was too overwhelming, and just when I thought my brain was going to explode with information overload, we turned a corner and beheld the most beautiful view I had ever seen. It was the deep blue ocean. The surface sparkled as sunlight hit the surface of the waves, which were bobbing about like creatures jumping out of the water. It was a breathtaking sight. I asked if we could stop by the ocean to picnic, but naturally the answer was no, and we drove away from the ocean and parked farther inland. I looked out of the back window as the immensity of the ocean disappeared behind some trees, and once again I hoped that the image would stay embedded in my mind.

About thirty minutes later, we took an extended break at a nice-looking rest area with a park. Jane and I went off to play for a while and get some much-needed exercise. Exhausted after a few minutes of being chased around by an evil Pinocchio, controlled by the hand of my sister, I settled back down in the van for a cup of tea. Most of the time, Mother was looking at the map, trying to figure out the best route to Iran. She had already decided which way we would go, but she was having second thoughts about whether to go to Russia or through Turkey to Iran. Either way, we still had to get to Yugoslavia, which was planned for that night, but Mother decided she would sleep on the decision until the next day. We ended up spending the night there at the rest stop in Italy.

Chapter 4

Yugoslavia

The next morning, we made it to Yugoslavia. I was sleeping when we arrived at the border. Everyone else woke up at seven and had their morning tea. My mother tried to rouse me from my slumber, but I continued to lie in a state of drowsiness. I had played in the park the previous afternoon until bedtime and had worn myself out. Mother allowed me to finish sleeping on the back seat, which usually wasn't permitted while the van was in motion. I recall waking up briefly at the border but nothing much after that. I knew we had made it to the next country, and I was thinking about what the stamp would look like. A few hours later, Mother drove past Zagreb, where we were scheduled to take a rest. We reached an isolated area and parked up for the morning.

It took me a few minutes to wake up, but the smell of food cooking stimulated my taste buds, and before long, I was rolling up my bedding and stuffing it into its daytime home, which was a brown canvas bag with leather straps. My mother was cooking eggs and bacon on the propane stove and making tea. I exited the van, full of anticipation of what Yugoslavia had in store for me. I ran about fifteen feet away and viewed the surroundings. It looked the same in all directions; evidently, we were in the countryside. Crossing this border felt like turning another year older on my birthday: I knew I had achieved something, but I still looked and felt the same. I shrugged my shoulders and ran back to the van, where breakfast was being served. Before I could get the first bite of breakfast, Jane began chanting, "Sleepyhead, stayed in bed, sleep too long, and you'll be dead!" while chewing on a piece of toast.

"Oh! Nice song, James!" I ranted back.

"Call me names, call me James, I don't care, it's all the—" she rattled back at me before being interrupted by our mother.

"Now, stop it, both of you!"

"But she started it!" I blurted out.

"Seriously, stop! James, apologize to your sister for the sleepyhead thing now!" Mother ordered.

"You called her James too!" I laughed.

"Just apologize to each other now," Mother demanded, frustrated. "And stop talking with your mouth full! Did I not teach you any manners?"

"I was only joking," Jane said. "And besides, I don't need an apology from Jenny, because I like the name James better than Jane, so there!" She gave me a half grin and stuck out her tongue at me.

"Okay, then, let's hurry this up, because we have to get back on the road," Mother huffed.

Jane and I were always causing a stir, joking, laughing, and occasionally squabbling, but it was rare for us to have any real disputes. Jane managed to get under my skin that morning only because I was still tired. It was not even the content of her made-up tune that was annoying to me; it was the fact that she could be so witty all the time and come up with rhymes instantaneously. She was extremely articulate and had a flair for verbal creativity—two traits I lacked. Speech was not a strong point for me, but what I lacked in verbal skills, I made up for in imagination.

Soon we were packing up the van, ready to continue on. By now, Jane and I had breezed past the earlier events and were on laughing terms again. We did a last-minute check under and around the Dinosaur to make sure we had not forgotten any belongings and headed out. The next objective was to make it that day to Bulgaria. I wanted Bulgaria to be extraordinary because so far I was not impressed with Yugoslavia. Either I had slept through the good parts, or there was nothing to look at. I had not seen anything that was noteworthy enough to write about. Later, we did drive through a couple of small villages that looked really quaint. All the houses were built differently but displayed the same gray stone walls and red roofs. The roads and bridges matched the houses. I wanted to stay in a hotel in one of these villages, thinking that maybe I could then find something out about the place, but we needed to keep driving.

It felt like we drove for miles and miles before we finally arrived at a campsite that was awkwardly situated on the side of a hill. I was not confident that parking on what appeared to be an extremely steep hill was a good idea. I envisioned us tumbling down the side, with all our stuff bouncing about in the van and ending down below in a pile of broken metal, wood, and glass, with the huge green Tupperware bowl upside down, lid off, and sugar all over the road. Nevertheless, we parked at the very top. Looking down, I saw the entire camp with its rectangular parking sites made from cement cut into the hill like a staircase. Each plot had a neat row of trees set around it, giving the camper a feeling of privacy. From this vantage point, I could see that it was quite lovely after all. It was still overly steep for my comfort, but that evening there was a feeling of tranquility and peace as the sun set slowly over the Yugoslavian sky.

Day Seven, April 14, 1975

We woke up at seven. We did not have breakfast until nine. We just woke up, dressed and went to the nasty hole in the floor toilet. There were women in there watching us brush our teeth, and when they smiled at us they had none.

When we woke the next morning and exited the van, we were surrounded by strange women in drab clothing. They all looked the same, with black scarves draped around their heads, black skirts, black jackets, white socks, and black shoes. I could see their hairy ankles between their socks and the hems of their skirts. It was rather disturbing. They had more than a passing curiosity about us and followed closely wherever we went, even to the bathroom. We left that camp pretty abruptly, without breakfast. My mother opted to find a more aesthetically pleasing location to eat. We drove for two hours looking for a nice place, but there were mostly small farmhouses and villages that disappeared when we blinked. We saw no campsites or rest stops. The landscape was also depressingly dreary. We were all getting hungry, but my mother insisted that we wait until we found a good spot to park. Finally, we drove by some fields where tiny yellow bunches of cowslips were growing. Cowslips reminded us of the British countryside, so we drove into one of these fields and started to have brunch. Seeing as we had made good time, because Mother had been driving like a bat out of hell, we decided to stay a couple of hours and stretch our legs and relax. We had postcards that Mother had picked up at the border that we needed to write, so we spent the afternoon frolicking in the field, writing, and generally relaxing.

While I was looking through the postcards, Jane started to write one to our grandmother that she already picked out. I could not find a card that I felt was an honest representation of what I believed Yugoslavia to look like. All the pictures were of beautiful blue skies and oceans, or village people dressed in brightly colored clothing, and I had not seen any of that. Most of the scenery consisted of dry, grassy hills and little villages with gloomy abodes. I was still trying to make my choice when Jane announced she had finished her message to Nan. I could not believe it. I threw the remaining cards on the small table that had become our life and grabbed the card. I began reading it.

Dear Nan,

As you can see we are in Yugoslavia, I wanted to send you a card from Italy, but we did not stop. We arrived in Italy the night before last and we came over the mountains in a carrier train, as the mountain roads were closed.

We drove all day yesterday and when we got up this morning it was 7:00, by 7:45 we were at the Yugoslavian border, we only drove about ten minutes.

I will write again soon.

Lots of love,

from Jane.

All this time I had been spending hours, slowly writing short accounts of the trip so far in my journal. It took me ages trying to perfect my writing while taking notes or writing letters. Now here was Jane, who had written nothing the whole trip, finished with this postcard in less than a minute. I was truly staggered. Not wanting to spend three hours writing another postcard, I quickly grabbed the pen from Jane and added on the bottom of the card "and Jenny."

Around three in the afternoon, we started to pack everything up and get on our way. We still had a long way to drive to get to the next country on our list, which was Bulgaria, and the plan was to arrive there early that evening.

Day Seven, April 14, 1975

We found a nice place with cowslips to park. We did not have breakfast until ten. We wrote on some postcards. I wanted to go to the other end of the field to pick flowers, but Ma said I shouldn't.

We put away all the stuff. At four Ryan put the key in the ignition. The van started, but it did not move. The wheels were stuck in the mud. Ma took out some of the suitcases to take the weight off. We put sticks under the wheels, but it still did not come out. We tried to push it out, but it only moved back and forward a little bit. We tried to do everything to get it out, but it kept going further down. Ma didn't know what to do. Finally a man and a boy came and asked us something in their language. We said we did not understand them. The boy said Halo, and asked us if we were stuck first in his language and then in broken English. The man went and found pieces of wood that he put under all the wheels. Everyone pushed the van. We did that for a long time changing the wood in all different ways. When the van did get out of the hole it was seven thirty. Ryan and Ma are so worn out they look like they are going to die. When the van was back out on the gravel road we put the cases back in the van. Now we are on our way to Bulgaria.

That was one of the worst days so far. Even though France had been freezing, we did not ache then as much as we did after pushing the Dinosaur for hours. We made it a point that we would never park in a newly ploughed field again, no matter how many flowers there were or how pretty it appeared. It was already late in the day when we started off again.

Day Seven, April 14, 1975. Second entry.

Today I was tired … I forgot to look at the stamp!

The next day, we were up bright and early as usual. We set off around eight and began the next part of the trip that would take us to Bulgaria. My mother was still indecisive about the route she wanted to take. Should we go through Romania and Russia to Iran or Bulgaria and Turkey to Iran? It was all too much for me. I just wanted to get wherever it was we were meant to be. In Belgrade, she had to make a choice, so she decided that we would go to Bulgaria, and if she changed her mind while there, we could detour north to Romania, around to Russia, and back down to Iran.

One of the variables Mother had not anticipated while planning the trip was the weather, which obviously caused problems and setbacks while in France. The same kind of weather conditions were reported in northern European countries. Since we might run into extreme cold weather again if we traveled to Russia, it was decided that Turkey would be the best route after Bulgaria. Soon we were back on track and driving on with a definitive plan of action.

We made it to Nis, where we took a break. This was more than likely the last major town we would pass through while in Yugoslavia, so we had to mail our postcards from here so the postmark would match the country. It was one of those all-important details that had to be done correctly. Mother had not written to Nan yet, so she grabbed a card and wrote a quick note. She picked the postcard that had all the colorful village folk standing in a line. I remember thinking that those people were a lie, as I had not seen anyone dressed like that, but I figured it didn't really matter after all. Before taking the mail to the post office, I had a quick nose at the postcard to see what Mother had written.

Dear Mum,

We are now in Yugoslavia at the moment. We hope to drive through Istanbul today. When we arrive, I will write a letter. We managed to get through Italy without any trouble, but we got bogged down in a field here. It took us four hours to get out!

Love from Elizabeth

Not impressed with Yugoslavia, I had very little to add to my journal, except to express my indifference to the country, I added a short comment.

Day Eight, April 15, 1975

We are still in Yugoslavia. It all looks the same. We are going to Bulgaria. Maybe it will be different there.

After the field ordeal, I was not interested in writing much. The trip had been full of trouble so far. Although my mother was really determined, I was not sure that the rest of us were, but we had no choice but to hang in there. Soon we started on our way to Bulgaria. To keep our morale up, all we could do was look to the future, when we would be in the sun and on sandy beaches. To keep my mind off the trip as much as I could, I decided to read one of the books that I had brought with me, called *The Three Billy Goats Gruff*. By early evening, we were driving through some mountains that were by far much safer than the Alps. There was no snow, so the roads were not slippery, and no snow meant there were no avalanches. I felt safe. I drifted off to sleep, only to be awakened by the van stopping abruptly some time later. I heard my mother and Ryan talking.

"Well, what are we going to do?" I heard Ryan say.

"I don't know. We can't drive over it," my mother said accusingly.

"Maybe we can get around it. It might not move," Ryan whispered.

When I opened my eyes, it was almost dark. The windows of the van were open. It was unusually humid outside. I rubbed my eyes and went to the front of the van, where my mother and Ryan were just sitting in their seats, staring out at the road. Still waking up, I expected to see a bear or something else really bad out there. Instead, sitting in a large, muddy, pond-sized hole blocking the middle of the mountain road was the biggest toad I had ever seen in my life, just staring into the headlights. The toad let out an awful growling noise every time it croaked. I never heard anything like it before. The frogs in England never sounded that threatening. I imagined the toad would speak and tell us we could not pass until we brought small children for it to eat. Since I was the only child there, the idea was not comforting. I rubbed my eyes to make sure I was not dreaming. At first, I found it to be menacing, but as I started to completely wake up, reality crept back into the recesses of my mind, and I accepted it for what it was: just a big, fat toad. I thought it was actually cute and wanted to get it as a pet. As expected, the toad was not going to be an immediate member of the family. After about a minute of being hypnotized by this massive amphibian, Ryan clambered out of the van. He went to the edge of the water and plopped his foot in. One splash and the toad took a gigantic leap and disappeared into the wilderness. With a triumphant smile on his face, Ryan reentered the van. With that, my mother drove around the edge of the hole as carefully as she could. Fortunately, we did not fall in, which I was fully expecting, considering our previous encounters; however, this time we escaped unscathed and trundled on toward Bulgaria.

Within an hour, we were almost at the border. We took a break along the side of a quiet road. It was nighttime by now, and I had an odd feeling that we were being watched from the darkness that surrounded us. Despite the hour and the spooky environment, Mother lit up the stove and began to boil water to make tea. Usually at night, I was asleep. I very rarely saw what it looked like, but this night I did. The country road we were parked on was not lit, and I couldn't see very well. I could tell we were by some big trees, and not knowing what was out there, I started to get paranoid. A spine-chilling shiver went through my body, even though the temperature was mild. As I looked out at the dim beams of light radiating from the van's headlights, I saw a flock of tiny birds fly by really fast. When I alerted my mother to take a look, she told me they were bats, not birds. I passed on stretching my legs or taking a pee behind a shrub in the pitch black. The last thing I wanted was a flying rodent with sharp teeth to get stuck in my long hair.

About half an hour later, we left. Fifteen more minutes went by, and I really needed to pee. Mother was clearly annoyed. She reminded me that we had already taken the break, and I should have gone when we were there. Flustered, she told me to take the top part of an empty three-tier cookie tin, do what I had to do in there, put the lid on it when I was done, and dispose of the contents at the next stop. At first I was not thrilled, but considering I could either wait for who knew how long or pee my pants, I reluctantly used the receptacle. The tin became my own personal Porta-Potty from then on. Although I was grateful that I could do my thing, it kind of seemed redundant, because a few minutes later, we were booking into a motel. Earlier that day, my mother had suggested that Ryan and she take turns driving to Bulgaria. They would keep up this trend until we reached Turkey, and then we would get a hotel room and take a good rest. But because they were already tired from the exhausting workout in the field, they thought better of it and pulled into a small motel for the night. We would not make it to Bulgaria that day after all.

Chapter 5

Bulgaria

After a good night's rest, we hurried forward with the morning formalities and began on our way to Bulgaria. We arrived at the Yugoslavia/Bulgaria border in no time at all, maybe an hour at the most. The routine was becoming familiar: show passports and visas, check the van for illegal possessions, stamp, and be on our way. We crossed the border and parked to run the "new country" errands. Ryan and Jane went off to change the remaining dinars into Bulgarian levs, and my mother and I went to find provisions. While we were at the counter, waiting to pay for our goods, the shopkeeper came over and gave my mother some cute wooden bottles in the shape of towers that contained tiny glass vials of rose oil. They smelled really good. We had been in this new country for only five minutes, and people were giving us gifts. They were the first souvenirs that we had from any country. I wanted them, but they were given to my mother. She let me look at them, but that was it. I remember being upset about that.

While we were there, interacting with the locals, my mother started talking to the border patrol. She asked them what they thought of the routes to Iran, just to verify that she had made the correct choice. They suggested that we go through Turkey, as it was safer and would cut time and mileage. I was glad, because Jane had told me that somewhere in the northern countries near Romania and Russia was a country called Transylvania, and I did not want to go there. The stories Jane told me about the people in Transylvania were not good, so I definitely preferred the Turkey idea.

After all the important chores were completed, we met up at the Dinosaur, climbed in, and went on our way to Sofia. Determined to keep to the scheduled meeting in Iran, Mother said that we were going to drive straight through Bulgaria, making only a few essential stops.

Because we would not be there very long, I wanted to take in as much information about Bulgaria as I could. I began to pack every small detail that was humanly possible into my brain. I wanted to be able to express in my journal how the country felt, what the most noticeable changes were, and anything that stood out above all else.

Day Nine, April 16, 1975

The areas have started to look a lot different than in England. Buildings are different, people are different, their clothes are different, and even food is different. Everything is really interesting. We stopped off at a town and a man in a shop told me about Macedonians, Ottomans, Byzantiums, and Romans. They are mostly dead now, but some of them are still alive.

When we stopped in tourist towns for items such as water and bread, the locals told us stories about how their town or city came about. Much of the talk revolved around the vast differences in architecture, in which I had begun to take an interest. A man with a very thick accent told me that many of the buildings of particular relevance were built hundreds of years ago by people who were all dead now, but they still lived in many surrounding countries. That confused me, but I was sure that with the unfamiliar accent and all, I had misinterpreted what I heard. Ancient civilizations were a mystery to me. I had never even heard of many of the people, and I wondered where they were. I couldn't understand how they could be all dead and living somewhere at the same time. Still, I knew I had much to learn. The idea of history had never meant that much to me, but now, as I was experiencing it, it became more compelling.

We took a brief walk to a nearby square. In the middle of this square was a tall obelisk. A plaque stated that it had been there since Anno Domini 350. The obelisk looked new to me, and I had a hard time believing it was true. Other than some of the outrageous claims about the ages of the monuments, and people being dead and alive, the Bulgarian people were very agreeable. So far, the Bulgaria experience was rather nice.

On the way to the next town, we saw a mass of interesting landmarks. There were ancient Roman ruins. I had never seen anything like them before. Believing that these ruins were built hundreds of years ago was easier than with the previous monument, given that these were broken and looked old. After seeing them, I was beginning to string together the concept of history, and Bulgaria, being located at the center of many previous super cultures, had plenty of it. I had so many questions, but we had no time to get the answers to them. After this eye opening stop, we were on our way to the town of Plovdiv, and another town was marked off the long list.

During the days, Jane and I would make up stories and tell them to each other. We had a lot of spare time to conjure up weird and unusual scenarios and jokes. Usually, after Jane had finished telling me some ridiculous, scary tale that I believed, I started on a "But what if?" rant. My mother would tell me that nothing bad was going to happen and everything was fine. She warned Jane not to put ideas in my head, as it was not good for me. If I started getting too freaked out, my mother would tell me to close my eyes and think of something that made me happy. Jane would turn everything around and begin goofing off and saying silly things to make me laugh. We began one day by looking at maps of where we had been and where we might go. It was another way for us to track our progress and pass the time while on the road. There were indeed some strange names out there, and Jane started naming some off.

"Oh, look, we could go through Greece," Jane said.

"Grease? Why would anyone call their country Grease? It sounds nasty!" I answered.

"No, not that kind of grease. It's spelled different, anyway," she informed me. "No, it would be better just to stick to Turkey. Ma, what do you think?" she asked.

Mother just kept on driving, not saying a word.

"We will probably just go straight through to Iran," Jane said next, pointing to Iran on the map.

"Well, I think all these names are dumb. Why call a country Turkey? Are there turkeys there?" I asked.

Jane put the map away and rolled her eyes at me. She started reciting an improvised story about how I was Hungary and how she gave me a Turkey with Greece, but I was afraid of it so Iran away. I was giggling in no time. She came up with an eclectic variety of absurd jokes about turkeys, which had me in a hysterical uproar. Undoubtedly, the trip was getting to us. Evidence from my journal clearly shows that I had mental states of sheer nonsense.

Day Nine, April 16, 1975

Tomorrow we go to Turkey. Turkey is a funny bird. We almost went to Hungary, and if we wanted to we could spent twenty minutes in Greece. Jane and I have been making turkey jokes. If an avalanche was a monster, what would it look like? (I drew a monster in my journal.) It looks like Frankenstein. Ha ha ha he he he I am going to Tur-key.

Looking at the map, it was possible that we could go through a small northern part of Greece to make it into Turkey. My mother was not sure if we could go into Greece, as she had not applied for visas to go there. Not knowing whether we needed them, she decided to go farther north and into Turkey, thus avoiding another country that really wasn't necessary. I was somewhat disappointed, because I had heard that Greek people had built many of the ancient ruins that we had seen. I had the idea that if we went to Greece, I would see men wearing white robes and sandals standing in front of huge boulders, crafting ruins, but now I would not get to see them. From Plovdiv, we drove past Harmanli and on toward the Turkish border. Two more sub-names were now crossed off the list. We had about another twenty-five miles to go before we entered the next country.

We stopped at an exceptionally small village set in the middle of some large fields, to get some fresh food items before continuing on to Turkey. A strange mist surrounded the place. I assumed it was because the humidity was high there. As I looked more carefully, I was not certain that this place was really a village, but instead more of a small farm community. The houses were all very tiny; their walls were made of large, irregular, dark gray stones, and they had thatched roofs. We drove slowly past a row of small buildings. Two elderly people sat outside a café. They sat oddly still, staring off into space. When we drove past them, their heads turned slowly as they watched us go by. We saw no shops of any kind, so we decided to park and walk around to find out where the stores were. By the time we had all exited the van, a few of the people from the village had gathered around. They were dressed in drab clothing that reminded me somewhat of the women we had seen in Yugoslavia, but these folk were not smiling. A tall, thin fellow walked across from the café and approached us. By this time, we were huddled together in front of the van, surrounded by these daunting villagers, who were looking perturbed that we had stopped there. The gentleman from the café was dressed a tad better than the other locals and had short, slicked-back hair. He walked up to Ryan and made eye contact. I noticed they were the same height. Ryan just stood transfixed, as if hypnotized.

"Can I hilp you?" the tall man said in a thick Bulgarian accent.

It would have sounded cool, as I had an affinity for accents, but it reminded me of a similar character who went around biting people's necks. I wondered momentarily if we were lost and had traveled too far north. I remembered the bats in Yugoslavia and the story of the ancient ones who were dead but still lived, and now here we were, in this sleepy town in the middle of nowhere. I stood as still as possible, mimicking the ancient obelisk, so I wouldn't be noticed. I was brought out of my paranoid state by my mother's voice. Fearlessly she stepped between Ryan and the Bulgarian man, breaking their gaze.

"Yes, sir. We are looking for a shop to buy bread and milk," she said adamantly.

"Ah, yes. Follow me, follow me," the tall man said, smiling and gesturing for us to go along with him. I tried to see past his smile at his teeth, but he broke of his grin before I could tell what they looked like.

As he led us toward the café, the village folk went off in different directions and skulked back from whence they came. In the back of my mind, I felt that this was a trap to lure us into an underground cave where we would get the life sucked out of us. When we entered the café, we saw that it actually served as the dairy, bakery, and local grocery store. The man explained that the village was so small that they had no need for more than what the café offered. He also mentioned that very few people traveled off the main road to go there; most travelers stopped at Harmanli. While politely informing us that we were idiots for being off the beaten track, he nicely packaged eggs, bread, and milk at our request. When he told Mother how much it was, she looked at her money to find that it was just a few levs short of the total. The man said it was no problem and gave us the items at a discounted rate. We thanked him graciously and left for the van.

We drove up the small street, but it turned out to be a dead end. After carefully maneuvering the Dinosaur back around, we drove slowly past the café and the tall man, who was standing outside. He watched and waved at us as we departed the creepy old village. Mother did not want to bolt away and be impolite or appear as if we were afraid of this strange place, so she drove away at a snail's pace.

When we turned on to the main road, I asked Jane if that had been Dracula. She looked at me as if I had just been released from a psychiatric ward.

"What?" she said.

"I said was that Dracula, one of the ancient people that are still alive?" I retorted with concern.

"Don't be so stupid. Of course it wasn't Dracula!" Jane said with an all-too-familiar roll of her eyes. "Just because he sounded different, it doesn't mean he's a vampire," Jane said reassuringly.

"But he could have been?" I said, believing there was still a chance it was him.

There was a brief moment of silence while Jane contemplated a logical answer to my moronic question. The whole time, she stared at me with this look that told me she felt sorry for me for some strange reason. She kept shifting about and making huffing sounds while keeping eye contact.

"Okay. There are no such things as real vampires. It's a myth, a story!" Jane said, getting impatient with me.

"That is not true," I said. "A man in one of the towns told me about Macedonians, Ottomans, and Romans, ancient people who still live in different countries in the world right now!" I said indignantly, overemphasizing the word "live."

Jane sat there staring blankly at me. Very slowly, a tongue-in-cheek smile came to her face. I was still waiting wide-eyed for the brilliant explanation she had for that. I sat back and crossed my arms in anticipation of her response. I started to feel like there was something I was not getting, as she wouldn't speak, and she looked like she was holding back a laugh. Finally, she composed herself. I was still waiting.

"Look," she said, sighing. "The ancient people are dead and gone. The ones who still live are their descendants. The Romans are from Italy. They live in Arr-Oh-Em-Eee, Rome! The Ottomans are probably the Turkish. I don't know what the Macedonians are, but they are not vampires, okay?" she said, sounding like a schoolteacher.

She shook her head and looked like she was about to laugh again. I contemplated her response for a few minutes and surmised that it was probably the truth, as Jane usually was really smart about those things and would never lie to me. But in the back of my mind, the Macedonians still seemed suspicious.

After the creepiness faded away and the village was way out of viewing range, we began to pick up speed. We had barely reached forty miles per hour when we heard a siren coming from behind us. I looked back to see that it was the police. At first, my mother did not realize they were pulling us over, but when they did not pass, it became evident that they were. When they approached the van, Mother asked what the problem was. They said that she was speeding. They informed her that the speed limit was fifty. Mother told them that she was only going forty. Trying to dispute their accusations did not change their minds, and Mother didn't come up with any crazy comebacks to get us out of the situation, so we were fined on the spot. Because we had just given our last lev away to Dracula, we had no money to give them except for foreign currency. The police saw our situation, realized we were telling the truth about the money, and let us off with a warning. We drove away at thirty miles an hour until we finally arrived at the Turkish border, an hour later than expected. While driving past a speed limit sign, it occurred to Mother that the speed limit was probably in kilometers and not miles, which meant we had indeed been moving at least sixty kilometers per hour. From then on, we made it a point to watch the kilometers and not the familiar miles per hour.

Chapter 6

Turkey

The weather had changed dramatically since our adventures in France. It was much warmer and the air somewhat drier as we rolled up to the Turkish border. When we arrived, the familiar procedures took place. We stayed longer than usual at this checkpoint, but not because anything unexpected or scary happened. In fact, the van check was quick, and unlike the border patrol in France, these inspectors were completely disinterested in our sugar and spices. I was glad that we didn't have to go through any Steve McQueen comments, since that quite honestly continued to be a tad bizarre to me. Still, I had to trust that Mother had good intuition when it came to people, as it had worked. Quickly trying to get that picture out of my head, I started thinking about what the stamp would look like. This would be the fifth border we crossed.

Once we had gone through the approval process, we were given our stamp, and we ventured onto the Turkish side of the border. I was permitted to view the stamp, which was really cool. The farther away from England we were, the more interesting the stamps became. The writing started to look different and appeared more like art, something worth looking at, probably just because it was unfamiliar to me. Satisfied with our collection of stamps so far, I returned the passport to my mother, and we began the routine of gassing up the van, changing currency, and buying provisions.

At this border, there were all kinds of travelers. It was quite a bustling place, with people from all over the world changing money and buying souvenirs and their own personal kinds of provisions. Cigarettes were apparently quite the craze. It seemed that everyone smoked, as many stocked up on large quantities of cartons to take on their journeys. We saw hitchhikers who actually walked on foot everywhere with rucksacks and bedrolls on their backs. There were people who wanted rides to the next town over, and some wanted rides all the way into India. We had to refuse a few requests ourselves due to the limited passenger space in the van. We met several British tourists who were going to the same places as we were, except their schedules did not match up exactly with ours.

We met a very charming British doctor and his wife. They were traveling to India to visit acquaintances that their families knew through more than a couple of generations of military service and merchant trading. He said things like, "In the 1700s, my ancestors began the first legal trading with India under the Honorable East India Company! Much later, my great-great-grandfather was a prominent general in the Royal ..." He would rant on with pride in his voice. Even though his stories almost put me to sleep, I liked him. He and his wife, June, were a really nice couple whom we learned had the surname of Sotheby. After listening to a few family stories, we agreed to travel with them along some of the same routes that we were planning to take. The Sothebys' vehicle was also a Volkswagen, but it was white and orange and had a fancy roof that expanded upward and out to make the camper bigger. It was really cool. I secretly wished our vehicle was like theirs, so we could have a few more feet of living space!

Another group of English people owned a completely white Volkswagen camper. I guess that was the vehicle of choice for many folks back then. Faith, Patrick, and Keith were younger than the doctor and his wife, and their interests were travel and photojournalism. They were traveling around specifically to record details of the Middle East and South Asia. They brought a variety of really nice cameras, tripods, and glass filters, and a mass of film. Keith had traveled on foot originally but decided to get a ride as far as India. Faith and Patrick had said he could go with them. I liked Keith because he said I acted more like eleven instead of nine, which made me feel all grown up. Plus he gave me a weird denim fishing hat to wear. At first, I didn't want to put it on because it looked funny to me, but he said my brains might fry in the heat if I didn't wear it, so I put it on immediately. Eventually I became very fond of the brain-protecting garment. Anyway, like the good doctor and June, Faith and her friends were heading in the general direction of India. It appeared that we would have traveling companions for at least some portions of the trip. The journey was quite lonely, so any people we met, if only for a brief amount of time, were really appreciated and meant a lot.

Before we left the border, we let the Sothebys know we were ready to go. They too were prepared to leave, and before long, we were on our way. As we took off, I waved good-bye to Faith, Patrick, and Keith and hoped we would see them again down the road. They were not going to Australia or any particular destination; they were just exploring different countries. At the time, I wondered why anyone would want to go miles away from home just to go through the types of situations that we went through, especially as much of it was not that pleasant. We met many kinds of people who traveled around for all kinds of reasons and sometimes no reason at all. It was something that some people did. I had yet to understand, but it was what it was. As long as nothing else scary, unexpected, or weird happened, it was fine by me. I considered the last two countries we visited and noticed a positive trend. They had both been pretty much uneventful, apart from getting stuck in the field, being challenged by an oversized amphibian, being besieged by hairy, toothless women, and the Dracula event. Well, at least nothing had been life-threatening. I hoped that these problems would not be repeated. I was now looking forward to seeing how different Turkey was from the rest of the world. So far, each country had subtle changes that one would not really notice right away, but I found that to be exponential. The farther we traveled, the more dramatically different were the cultures. It was not just language, clothing, and food differences, either. The whole atmosphere started to feel different: the new mentalities, the dry air, even the smell, and especially the heat. I thought of France and wondered which extreme was more unbearable.

Our van didn't have air conditioning, so during most of our driving time in the hot countries, the windows were open. I was quite overheated, but against my mother's advice, I would not take off the sweater I was wearing. I had taken four favorite winter tops with me. They were exactly alike except for the colors, which were purple, orange, lemon, and pink. I wore those clothes constantly, and while in the cold countries, I really appreciated them. Obviously, by now it was time to pack them up, but they were my favorites, and I refused to part with them, so naturally I was extremely uncomfortable during my bouts of stubbornness. Generally, I was a reserved, quiet child, but the trip was changing me. It was a psychologically altering experience. I just wanted to be where we were supposed to be in Australia. But the journey was inevitable, so forward through Turkey we went.

Day Ten, April 17, 1975

Today is Thursday. We made it to Turkey. There are no Turkeys here. It is really hot. Ma told me to take off my pink sweater, but I don't want to.

From the Turkish border, we drove through Havsa, Luleburgaz, and Curlu. Every time Jane and I were allowed to cross off a town on the list, it felt like we were close to completing our goal, much like viewing the stamps. During the drive, Faith caught up with us, and for a while, all three vans were driving in a Volkswagen convoy. I thought it was really great that we had driving company. I made funny faces and acted like a clown at our new friends through the window. They probably thought I was a lunatic, or at least mentally challenged. Eventually, when my mother noticed what I was doing, she told me to stop. Jane thought it was funny too, although she didn't make faces at them.

Eventually, we made it to Istanbul. This city was big. It was a massive version of the border town, with tourists, hitchhikers, and local people walking around everywhere. The buildings were all different too. Some looked the same as in England, France, and Italy, and others looked like the wooden towers that my mother was given in Bulgaria. Most of the time when I saw new or different buildings I had no idea what they were used for. I knew that many were homes or offices and some were museums, but a large majority of the more unusual buildings were places of prayer. We drove by a huge mosque, which I had been told at the border was a hard-to-miss building. That was so true. It did baffle me, though, because I had been told it was the Blue Mosque, and this mosque was white and gray. There was no other gigantic mosque around, so I assumed I was looking at the correct one. There were other, smaller mosques, and they were all remarkable, but none were blue.

I couldn't believe how different it was here. The driving was different too. The vehicles moved in a less organized manner, and the noise of honking horns and people shouting in their native tongue at each other was insane. It was unsettling, but even more disquieting than all that cacophony was the sound that would suddenly emanate from seemingly nowhere. It was like a siren, except it was a male voice. I was told it was the call to prayer coming from the mosques, and promptly I had a brief lesson on the Muslim religion. I wondered why Christians or Catholics did not deliver the word of God out loud as well or call to their followers. I thought that if Turkey permitted Muslims to shout prayers across the land, then they would allow all religions to practice the same method of preaching, but apparently only Muslims did this. In a way, I was glad, because the sound actually troubled me. After the prayer call stopped, sometime later I felt I could take a breath. This city by far was the most different we had experienced up to this point.

While my mother tried to maneuver the van through traffic to get out of Istanbul, we came to a stop in the middle of an extremely busy road. Two disgruntled locals were battling it out verbally for the right to pass into a lane. While we waited patiently for them to end their dispute, some small boys came up to the window. They were speaking their language, repeating the word "baksheesh," which meant nothing to us, so at first the reason for their communication was uncertain. After "baksheesh" did nothing for them, they started gesturing with their fingers to their mouths like they wanted cigarettes, and sure enough, they did. At first, my mother said no and tried to shoo them away, mostly for their safety, as they were now clambering about the van. The traffic started moving, as the two disputing men had now made friends and were driving forward; however, we could not move, because of the children. Ryan tossed a few cigarettes out the window, and the children soon moved on. Mother glared at him, but it suddenly became apparent why so many people at the border were stocking up on cigarettes. No cigarettes, no passage. The cheeky little rascals also begged for matches! At first, I thought that maybe some adults had asked the kids to get cigarettes for them, but as we drove away, I looked back and saw these boys younger than I light up. It was unbelievable. My mother and Ryan didn't even behave like it was wrong, which baffled me, because I can guarantee that if I had picked up a cigarette and started smoking it, my butt would have been smoked! I remembered the "when in Rome" line Mother had told me. From my history lesson in Bulgaria, I knew that the Romans went everywhere, not just Italy, so the saying applied for this country too. Regardless of the differences between cultures, I still could not believe that parents would let their children ask for cigarettes like that, no matter what country we were in.

By now, the Volkswagen convoy had been separated during all the wild driving on the hectic streets. We lost track of the Sothebys and Faith's crew. I looked out of the window and through the crowds of cars and pedestrians, but I couldn't see either van. Both parties were gone. I was disappointed, and I hoped we would meet back up with them soon. As fascinating as Istanbul was with all its new noises, mosques, and diverse people, I was glad to be driving away from there. Our next stopover was going to be at Ankara, which was about two hundred and fifty miles away, taking into account the winding of the mountain roads. We first had to cross a large river called the Istanbul Strait. Originally, I possessed no concerns about crossing this river, as I assumed it would be the same as so many others we had previously driven over; however, I realized I was incorrect in my belief when we arrived there. It was huge, more like an ocean than a river to me.

The idea of crossing this immense mass of water by the newly built Bosphorus Bridge was terrifying. One would have thought that with all the mountain ranges we'd traveled on so far, height would not be a fear factor. It is remotely possible that experiencing such heights also triggered the fear, as the bridge appeared extremely menacing from our vantage point. The bridge looked to be up in the sky, where maybe aircraft should be. I am certain now that my overactive imagination must have made it appear so elevated. Nonetheless, here it was, and people were using it. The bridge had been open for only two years, and I was convinced it would not hold the weight of all those cars, trucks, and vans. The mountains we traveled on had been bad, but that bridge looked much worse. After a family discussion, we decided to go for the newly scripted option B and cross by ferry. Apparently, I was not the only one who thought the bridge looked somewhat intimidating. I thought that if I did have to cross the bridge, I might close my eyes and think of something funny to make it better, but every time I did that, I fell asleep and ended up missing hours of the trip. This time, though, even my mother could not think of anything funny enough to go that route.

We waited near the dock for quite some time to get tickets and finally board the ferry, but it was nothing we could not handle, considering some of the setbacks we had experienced so far. The ferry was much like the one we had taken from England to France, except the view was so much nicer. When we left the dock, we could see everything up and down the river. It was a truly spectacular view, and for the first time, it felt like a vacation moment instead of a heavy task. That did not last long, though, and before long, we were driving off the ferry and continuing on our way to Ankara, the capital city of Turkey.

Ankara was magnificent. I had thought that Istanbul was diverse, but Ankara was even more so. You could look one way and see a structure that looked like it came straight from a sleepy town in Yugoslavia or look another way and see a beautiful mosque with minarets stuck about the sides. On the subject of minarets, it was not long before we heard the call to prayer again. Even though the prayer song was supposed to be godly, there was never a time that the sound did not scare me half to death. Another subject that was integrated as part of my educational experience on this trip was religion. The few details I learned about the individual beliefs started to contradict the meaning of God for me. I began thinking that religions were designed just to control the masses. My reasoning was that God would not make up different rules for all people, because that would cause chaos. I believed in one god that did not lay down ground rules based on what the weather was like. My mother always taught me to be open-minded about such matters and allowed me to be a free thinker. She explained that she was brought up with the religious background of the Church of England. My father was a Buddhist, and one of the first conversations regarding religious belief stemmed from their differences. I had no problem with what individuals wished to base their lives on, but I found the constant sound of Muslim prayer call to be extremely bothersome, especially as not everyone who lived in Turkey was a Muslim. Surely, I thought, if the Muslim people were so devout, they wouldn't have to be reminded to pray. Still, this was just another subject that I had to put in the back of my mind for a later date, until we dealt with the mission at hand.

We were supposed to make a night stop at Ankara, but due to the time we spent at the border and the short delay in Istanbul waiting for the ferry, my mother decided we would just make a quick stop: eat, refuel, bathroom, and back on the road. We seemed to have a "delay and dash" strategy. Despite these stop-and-go interruptions, we always managed to make it to our destinations on time, and that was the goal now: making it to Iran on time to meet Fiona and Todd.

The route from Ankara to Iran was a winding, mountainous drive. At first, Jane and I were all eyes on the road to look for interesting things, but as time went on, the road started to look pretty much like any other rocky mountain trail. The cities were gone, and the scenery was bland. The roads up here did not appear to be standard tar or asphalt covered, either. They were more like cement and gravel and were slightly narrower than usual. There were only a few barriers on the outside edge to keep you from falling off the side, so if you were not careful, that was where you would end up. At some points, we had to squeeze over to one side so vehicles traveling the opposite way could pass. Many times, the direction we were driving in placed us on the outside edge of the mountain road, so when we had to squeeze over to let someone pass, we were in danger of tipping down and over the edge. When I looked out the van window, I could see down the mountain to other looping roads and see all the seemingly small cars riding on them. At one point, we were so close to the edge that some of the small rocks and stones plummeted over and down the steep embankment onto other roads. Falling rocks and occasional landslides were also possible, so we heard. It was quite dramatic. It was too much for me, so I closed my eyes to think of something better. Before long, I fell asleep.

When I woke up, it was nighttime. Mother was driving furiously along the meandering roads that incidentally did not have any streetlamps to illuminate the path ahead. This had actually been the norm since the mountains in Bulgaria, but we usually traveled the mountains by day and had not encountered these conditions since France, which had mostly been lit up by the snow anyway. In addition, these mountains possessed very few plants or trees. The mountains were, for the most part, just solid rock, and there wasn't anything, not even a tree or shrub, to reflect light off to get a perception of depth.

We now had a new harrowing situation. Mother was getting tired, and Ryan didn't want to drive and possibly be the reason for our early demise. There were no visible villages or nomadic tribes set up anywhere. Finding a place to park for the night in the mountains proved to be a difficult task. Mother was driving frantically, because she had seen an eighteen-wheeler adorned with colored lights around the trailer and really bright headlights that lit up the road in front, far ahead up the mountain. The Dinosaur could barely light up six feet ahead of the road, making the drive extremely hazardous. I was actually afraid at this point, more so than when I had fallen asleep earlier. Knowing how close we had been to the edge in the daytime had been frightening, but now it was almost pitch black. I started encouraging my mother to drive faster, and I hoped that we could catch up with the huge truck. It was so bizarre trying to keep track of that vehicle. One minute, we could see it miles ahead, headlights blazing on the path before it, and then suddenly, the truck would curve off around a bend, and the lights would disappear. Only when we finally made it around the same bend did we spot the truck again. The positive side of the whole ordeal was that we were gaining on the truck pretty fast. Eventually, we caught up with what I had decided to call Rudolph and followed extremely close to its rear end. About thirty minutes later, the driver of the truck came to a stop. He pulled over to the side where there was presumably a spot where he could park for the night. He must have known the trail pretty well, as we could not see the edge of the road, or anything else, for that matter. Mother decided that if it was good enough for him to park there, we would park beside him. We would be safe, because if there was enough room for that huge vehicle to park, then there was enough space for us. Mother carefully passed the glowing red lights on the back of the truck and parked carefully to the right of it, leaving a gap of about a foot between us. She said that parking close to it would protect us from the high winds that could possibly push the van over the edge. It made sense to use that massive truck, at least five times our vehicle's size, for protection from the elements. We had been driving all day and pretty much all night. Mother was exhausted, and before long, we were all asleep.

The next morning, I was rudely awakened by the rocking of the van and the sound of Turkish children. I looked out the window to gaze upon nothing but mid-air. I quickly backed away from the window and alerted everyone to the quandary to our right. Everyone looked out to see that we had parked on the wrong side of the big truck. We were parked literally on the edge of the road, next to a steep drop. No one could exit through the driver's side door without falling to his or her death. Ryan jumped up and went to open the side doors, which were on the land side of the van. As he pulled the handle, it came off in his hand. With a confused look on his face, he bounded over to the front passenger side and went to open the front door. He saw that we were surrounded by children. They were laughing and shouting at us and rocking the van, which was extremely frightening. Panic-stricken, Ryan looked around and found some cigarettes, which he threw out the window. While the children groveled around on the ground to retrieve the cigarettes, Mother jumped into the driver's seat, turned on the van, and drove us quickly away from the edge of the mountain and the impudent rascals. She parked up ahead where it was all clear and stopped, jumped out of the van, and tried to free us from the vehicle. We all ended up having to clamber out the driver-side door, as the Turkish children—who, incidentally, had appeared from nowhere—had stolen all parts of the van that could be removed. They had taken the side-door handle and the back window handle. They had been trying to take off the bumpers and side mirrors when we woke up.

Fortunately, we escaped the malevolent meddling of the Turkish tykes and the peril of the mountain drop. Had we not woken up when we did, I am sure the kids would have knocked us over the mountainside.

Rudolph was nowhere to be seen and had probably taken off hours before us, as we didn't see him again. Even more bizarre was the fact that there were no camps, tribes, or towns for miles. We never found out for certain where the children came from, but there was a small village about twenty-five miles from where we had parked, and we surmised they could have been from there. Relieved that we had escaped from death on the mountain, we decided to take a rest at the village. While there, we changed from our bedclothes into our regular day clothes. The weather was hot and dry, but I still insisted on wearing one of my sweaters. My mother was telling me to change my clothes, but I distracted her train of thought by getting out my journal and pen to write. I felt that the events that had recently taken place were experiences worth recording, and I began writing. My mother stopped harassing me about the sweater and let me jot down my notes. When she wasn't looking, I took a peek in her ledger to see if I could find some interesting information to write about. It was all pretty boring. Spent nine thousand Lire here, spent ninety Din there, but the thing that caught my eye was the amount of miles we had travelled so far. Her last entry had us at two thousand five hundred miles away from our start point. Now that was worth writing about.

Day Twelve: 19 April, 1975

We almost went over the edge of a mountain and died. Some Turkish children stole our door handle and we could not get out of the van. We escaped from the deadly mountain. Today I am wearing my lemon sweater. I am keeping my clothes inside the van because I don't want my favorite sweaters to get taken. I was going to wear them all, but it was too tight and too hot. Ryan tried to fix the door and window handles with string. I saw somewhere that we have driven two thousand five hundred miles already. We must be almost back around the other side of the world already.

When we parked, we generally had a set amount of belongings that went outside the van to make room for dining. We put our shoes, individual suitcases with our clothes in them, and our bagged blankets on a tarp underneath the van at every long stop. My Porta-Potty tin went under the van too. Since Bulgaria, it had been a necessary item.

As long as what I had to do was not solid, I had the tin at my disposal. This would also be cleaned and stashed under the van during these breaks. Up to this time, we had no problem with anything going missing, but the children in Turkey were scoundrels. They took anything that they could get their hands on, which meant we had to be extra careful about watching our few belongings. Now we tried to make the stops as quick as possible to avoid the possibility of a chance encounter with pesky thieves. This was unlike the leisurely lunches we took in France and Italy. Mother would have us put our belongings under the van, and two stayed at base, while the other two went and searched for water. Then she cooked our lunch and tea on the gas stove. We ate, washed our dishes, got all our belongings back in the van, and took off again. We never left a mess and always took our trash with us until we could dispose of it properly. Mother would not have us disrespecting any country, no matter what the locals were like. This became routine.

This time, though, I was more watchful of my belongings. I was paranoid because I was a child too, and that might make the kids want to steal my stuff more. So far at this village, we did not see any juveniles trying to creep up on us. I deduced it was because they were all on the mountain that morning. While Mother and Ryan were tucking into their lunch, Jane and I started to look over the map again. We were heading toward Iran, Afghanistan, and Pakistan, and we started looking at that area of the map. It was not long before Jane started making silly comments about some of the names of the places again. Jane pointed to a town called Katmandu.

"Look, Jenny," she said, pointing to a small dot on the map. "Cat men do, you know!" She giggled.

"What do they do?" I said, looking at the map curiously.

"I don't know," she said, laughing. "Oh, here's a naughty one— La Hore," she said in a French accent.

"What does that mean?" I asked.

"Nothing!" She smirked back at me. "Oh, this is terrible. We have Bang Galore, but wait, we have some Luck now, that's good!" she said, her finger racing over all the different names.

I was desperately looking for a town or city name that I could change into something funny, but I was never as quick as Jane. Suddenly I saw one. I blurted out a sentence that broke up the word Islamabad. My mother almost choked on the mouthful of food she had in her mouth.

"Jennifer! Don't ever say that! I don't ever want to hear you say that again—you'll get us killed!" she said, trying to swallow and speak at the same time.

"But Jane was—" I started to say.

"Just put the map away now, and watch what you say," Mother said, still trying to swallow her lunch, and ending our briefly punny moment. I wanted to mention not speaking with your mouth full but thought better of it.

I could not understand why I was always the one who seemed to say or do something wrong or unacceptable. I had thought it was funny, but then it was explained that Muslims probably would not appreciate my silly humor. I really wasn't trying to insult anyone; I was just trying to make a joke out of a word like Jane. I kind of saw how it could look negative, but seeing as it was only meant as a pun, I wondered what the big deal was. Soon after the interrupted lunch, we were back on the road. Mother determined that she didn't want to stay too much longer in Turkey. Instead of taking breaks and stopping, she wanted to get to Iran that day.

My mother did most of the driving and took on the task through the dangerous routes. Ryan didn't mind driving as long as it was straightforward and not through a bustling city or through hazardous situations. With that in mind, my mother was again the designated driver. Procrastination was not on the agenda at this time, so she had to be hasty. This country, which Jane and I had mocked with its funny name and all, was turning out to be quite different from what I had thought originally. I actually had no real expectations for any of the countries we would visit, but what I did experience was not like anything I could have imagined. Certainly, never in a million years could I have thought of being in a van on the edge of a mountain surrounded by thieving, homicidal children. If anything, that ordeal was more like a nightmare.

Every country we visited had novel and unique attributes as well as new complications. Turkey was fascinating and frightening to me. I wondered just how different and just how scary the remainder of the trip would be. After all, we still had four more countries to visit before we took the boat over to Australia. I must have fallen asleep while contemplating what Iran would be like, because when I came to, we were still in Turkey. It seemed like we drove for an eternity, and we were still in the Turkish mountains. Just when I thought that we must have been driving in one huge circle, we spotted the Iran border.

Chapter 7

Iran

We made it through to Iran with no problems at the border, or so we all believed at first. There was always a feeling of apprehension as we approached a border, like we might get turned away or something. Even though these were irrational thoughts, because all legalities had been taken care of, it still felt weird. It was like having a cop car driving behind you, even though you know you have done nothing wrong. When we arrived at the border, Ryan, Jane, and I went off to change currency and get some drinks. It was so hot, and we were parched. Ryan usually went with my mother to the border checks, but she had asked him to accompany Jane and me to buy drinks. While we went to purchase items, my mother went to take care of the paperwork. We bought a whole bunch of bottled juices and water and joined Mother back at the van. She looked a bit troubled, and at first, we thought we had been turned away. But she assured us that everything was all right and ushered us to the van. We left pretty abruptly and began our drive to Tabriz. Mother was quiet the whole time and had a glazed look in her eyes, like she was going to cry. Later, we found out that the man handling our paperwork back at the border had taken her back to a room under false pretenses and wanted to handle more than paperwork. He had touched her inappropriately and told her that she was different from Iranian women, and that he liked her green eyes, dark red hair, and white skin. Fortunately, she managed to free herself from him before anything more serious happened, but she was still pretty shaken up. We made it a point from then on to stay together as a family, no matter where we went. My first impressions of Iran were not good, and already I had an idea why the country was called Iran. Still, the man at the border was just one person, and I would not judge a whole population based on one inhabitant. I was looking forward to spending time in Tehran with Minah and learning more about her people.

From the border, we rushed to the next location. Even though we had been trying not to stop for too long at any one place, my mother said that it would be better if we stopped at a hotel in Tabriz, so we could get properly cleaned up and reorganize the van, as we would be staying at Minah's house the next day in Tehran. I was getting excited about the prospects of seeing Fiona and Todd. A familiar face was something that I was desperate to see, even if it was strange old Fiona.

The night in Tabriz was uneventful, fortunately. Early the next morning, we were off once again, but before we left, we went to have a drive-by viewing of Iran's Blue Mosque. Somewhere along our travels, we had heard it was a well-respected historical piece of architecture that had survived since the 1400s. It had undergone some restoration a couple of years before because of earthquake damage that had occurred eons ago, and it had finally opened for the public to view. I was looking forward to seeing this mosque, and I hoped it really was blue, unlike the Blue Mosque in Turkey. When we drove by, I could see that it was indeed incredible, especially as it was so old and had survived so much, but it wasn't blue. It was red and brown. I began thinking that maybe it was not a literal meaning but a psychological one. Maybe when you felt blue, you went there to pray, and then you felt better. Who knew? It was another one of those things that I had to ponder at a later time.

We arrived in Tehran at about midday. The traffic there was unbearable, with the same stop-and-go approach as in Turkey. Jane and I had been drawing in the back of the van. We had pencils and pens that we were supposed to keep in a box, but I kept out the few colors I wanted to use and placed them on a shelf next to the back window. With all the stopping and going, the makeshift latch that Ryan had tried to make out of string on the back window sprang open. All the pens fell out onto the busy road. Jane rolled her eyes and said she would get them for me, as the stopping of the van usually lasted a few minutes at a time. She opened the side door and skipped out around the back to pick up the pens. I watched her out the back of the Dinosaur, and I was laughing.

All of a sudden, there was a break in the traffic, and Mother took off as fast as she could, taking advantage of the available space. Jane just stood there in the middle of all that chaotic traffic with the pens clutched in her hands and a panicked expression on her face. She tried to run toward us but kept getting stopped by cars coming from every direction. Horns were beeping and honking like mad at her to get out of the road. I screeched to my mother that Jane was out of the vehicle. At first, my mother was completely oblivious to what I was saying, probably thinking I was joking. I started getting hysterical, screaming about how the latch had popped open and the pens had fallen out, Jane had left the van, and on and on. Eventually, my mother looked in the rearview mirror and saw poor Jane running like crazy to get to us. Mother screeched to a halt. Cars were clanking all around, and the verbal abuse was probably quite profane. I can only imagine what they were shouting at us. Still, one of her own was missing in action, and she was not about to leave a man behind. Jane finally caught up to the van. She was out of breath, but at least she was safe, back in the van where she belonged. Mother was not angry, but she warned us not to do anything like that again. She told us to put away our drawing supplies anyway, because we would soon be at Minah's house. I felt terrible that it was my fault, and I don't think we drew much after that day. Jane and I stayed quiet and just waited until we arrived at the next stop.

The call to prayer was also common in Iran, and it had already started as we drove through the streets to get to the address that Fiona had given Mother. It took a while to find the house, but we finally made it. We rolled up to the driveway and happily bounded out of the van. It was so good to get out and stretch our legs after hours of being penned up. An old man there was taking care of a cute pet lamb. When he saw us, he tied the animal up and ran inside the building to let Fiona and Minah know that we had arrived. It was so good to see Fiona, but Todd had not come with her. She said that he had stayed at home in England to take care of Angel, as they couldn't bring her.

I had never met Minah, so I was apprehensive about the introduction. I had seen a picture of her, and I remembered that she was very beautiful and elegant looking. She was a born Iranian and was related to the shah. The four-story building we had driven up to was her home—the entire building. She had a swimming pool in her backyard that I was dying to take a swim in, but it had not been filled up, so that was a bit of a disappointment. I also wanted to pet the lamb, but I was not allowed to do that, either. The whole ordeal was all about the adults, and I was quickly getting quite bored.

Later that evening, we were shown to some living quarters on the fourth floor that we could stay in while visiting. We were scheduled to have dinner with our host, and I was told explicitly by Fiona to bathe, dress nicely, behave well at dinner, and not do anything to disrespect

Minah or her home. My mother had already taught me manners, so I was a little upset that Fiona would even think I would be anything but a perfect guest. The third floor was where the dining area, kitchen, and all the staff quarters were. Fiona led us to the dining room. There was a huge, long table with room for at least twenty people. I was put at the lower end of the table, which I thought was the head of the table. It made me feel special until Fiona told me that Minah did not like children very much, so I had been seated the farthest away from her end of the table, which was the actual head of the table. I sat there for what seemed like a millennium, and finally Jane and the other adults came in and seated themselves. I was looking at my mother and Jane for cues on what to do, but all I could feel were the sharp stabs coming from Fiona, who was glaring daggers at me. She was giving me the "you'd better behave" look. It was somewhat intimidating, and it made me feel uncomfortable. Minah entered the room and seated herself with the help of her staff, who politely pushed her chair in for her.

While the adults chatted for a while, the servers came out and gave us fresh water with ice in it. I was never so glad for a glass of water in my life. We had been cautious about water during the trip, so this was a treat. I gulped back the refreshing cold drink with enthusiasm. As I raised the glass, the ice clanked noisily onto my nose. From either side of the raised glass, I saw displeased stares coming from the adults. I realized right away what I had done and tried to play it off by politely putting down the glass and smiling sweetly. After a few seconds, they all went back to their chatter.

It seemed to me that dinner was taking forever, so I began to get fed up with waiting. Even Jane, who was usually funny and playful, was behaving like an adult. I was getting more and more impatient. I started swaying my legs back and forth on the huge chair that seemed oversized even for adults. Again, this gained me some attention that was not positive. I immediately stopped the swaying leg action, but I didn't know what to do with my hands. I could not lean my elbows on the table or touch anything, so I just put my arms to the sides and hoped that I was being good. After a while, the staff brought out the first dish. I was so relieved, and I felt I could finally move. The food had an unusual aroma that smelled different from anything I had ever eaten, but I was up to new food until I saw it. It looked like something I had seen growing in a pond in Italy while I was looking for frogs. I politely told the staff that I did not want it, and once again I received irritated glares from everyone. That alone told me I was being obstinate. Fiona was furious. She flew out of her chair, making a horrible scraping sound on the marble floor, and grabbed me by the arm, ranting on about how rude I was not to try new food and how I was being disobedient. Even my mother looked shocked, but she did nothing to stop the crazed woman. I hadn't realized that Fiona could move that fast, considering her mass.

She dragged me to the kitchen, where an ancient old man was. In fact, it was the same old man who had greeted us when we arrived. He spoke no English at all, but I was left in his charge. Fiona blurted something out in Farsi or English with a very irate Scottish accent, either way, the old man understood, and then I was stuck with him. I didn't even know that Fiona spoke Farsi, but apparently it was enough for him to understand that he had to look after me now. I was learning more and more about Fiona. Plainly, she had a lot of secrets, and a quick-changing personality to go with them. She thrust me toward the old man and turned to leave. I tried to run out of the kitchen and follow her lead, but the old man seized my arm and held it tight. He yanked me over to the counter, where he tried to push sugar cubes and warm goat's milk down my throat. It was horrible torture, but no one came to save me.

A couple of hours later, when everyone else had eaten, my mother came to get me. I cried when I saw her and told her what had happened. I tried to show her my arm, hoping it was bruised from the physical contact that I had experienced with both Fiona and the old man grabbing at my arm, but they were too good. They knew how to abuse without a bruise. My mother laughed it off and said I was exaggerating. I probably was, but it still felt like pain and suffering to me. On the way up to our room, she told me that if I had only tried the saffron spinach, then the situation would have been different. Saffron spinach sounded like such an innocent dish. I had never seen it before, and it looked kind of scary. Being a child, I thought that I would be excused from trying the meal, not excused from the table! Evidently, my punishment was no food at all. That evening, all I had consumed was sugar cubes and gross milk. We went up to the sleeping quarters, where I crashed almost immediately.

The next day, we went out and drove around the city to see some of the local sights. At first I was reluctant to go out driving. That was all we had done for weeks, but after carefully considering the alternative, I opted for the sightseeing event. This city was much like Turkey, except, like all the other countries, it had its own exclusive sights, scents, and individual conduct. Persians had all manner of vehicles that they used for daily life. There were people on foot and riding bicycles, mopeds, cars, and vans; and like Turkey, the rules of the road were unclear. Every motor vehicle had dents, scratches, and missing paint. My mother commented on the beaten-up vehicles and said that Iran probably didn't have car insurance, because it wouldn't be worth it. There were small collisions almost all the time. The drivers just screamed a few words at each other and drove on. Also, there were no limits on how many passengers you were allowed to carry in or on your vehicle. I saw a man drive by with a woman, two babies, and a large flat loaf of bread the size of a surfboard draped over the front of his moped. That was the most bizarre sight I had seen so far.

In awe of the size of the bread, we stopped by a bakery to see how they made it. The store was just a basic room with a huge clay oven. The dough was pounded out to enormous sizes on the stone floor and then cooked along the sides of the huge oven. The smell was divine, and the taste was even better. While we were staring at the bread-making procedure, one of the bakers gave us a sample of what we learned was called *taftoon*. For something that was prepared on the floor, the bread tasted really good. We bought a large slab, which was baked especially for us. The family-size *taftoon* barely fit through the van door. We had to turn the bread sideways to get it in. The whole ordeal cracked me up. That was one of the highlights of the day.

By now, we accepted the commonplace act of people begging for cigarettes and money. One of my mother's entries in her ledger was "gave beggars X amount of rials." I guess all monetary output was important to record, no matter how trivial it seemed. Even though there were incidents of adults begging, it was mostly children who came up to the cars with their incessant pleading. The most annoying adults were the traders who busily stuck their goods through the window and made offers right there and then. We had carpets come through the window, clothing, shoes, gold, and turquoise, among other items. We never bargained or bought anything through our window, though. Moving through all the walking merchants always held us up, as Mother did not want to run them over. We would creep along at a snail's pace for ages before we could make a break for it. Driving was a little better at the times of the call to prayer. We made a dash for it whenever we heard the mysterious voice calling out to the world.

The next time we heard the sound of prayer call chanting through the air, we decided to turn back and return to the house. A few hours of sightseeing were enough for us. As soon as I walked in through the door, the ancient one accosted me and lugged me up to the kitchen. Once again, I was given the sugar cubes and warm milk treatment. I believe he thought he was being nice, but I despised it. I scrambled away from him and ran to my mother, who was now talking to Minah. The lady was going to give my mother a tour of her house. She said I could come with them as long as I was quiet. I promised I would be, as I did not want to have to stay with the old geezer.

Minah took us to her floor and showed us her living quarters. It was a huge, luxurious place. Just as I was thinking that this woman must be a millionaire, she opened a huge closet that was stacked from the floor halfway up the wall with money of all different currencies, verifying my suspicions. On viewing the huge stash, I assumed it must have been the totality of the lady's money, but she nonchalantly told my mother that this was where she kept her spare cash. Minah closed the closet doors and went on to show us the rest of the house. Yes, it was beautiful. She told my mother that Allah had provided for her and that the next day she would take Mother to the Golden Shah Mosque where she prayed; she said that she could pray with her for a safe journey and a wealthy life. Minah said you could ask for anything at the mosque, and God would give. The next day was going to be exciting for my mother, but that was tomorrow, and this day was still young.

I spoke to Minah only once. I asked her if the mosque that she was taking my mother to see was really gold, because two other mosques that I had viewed that were supposed to be blue were not. At first she was puzzled, but then she showed me a picture of the Golden Shah Mosque. It was blue! I was so confused, but Minah politely explained to me that the dome was made of gold and turquoise, and much of the outside and inside was in fact gold. As for the Turkish and Tabriz mosques, they were called blue because the inside walls of both structures were covered in blue tiles. Finally, something made sense. Minah was so wise.

That was the only time I managed to have a conversation with Minah, as I had been banned from any contact with anyone except the old guy. I had to follow him everywhere while he did his chores. I hated it, but that was what I was told to do. I stayed with him until the evening, and then I was taken to the guest quarters, where I joined my family. They all had done something interesting that day, and they talked about this and that. One of the topics that had been discussed earlier that day involved one of the guests from that awful dinner party that I was banished from. Minah had asked for a meeting with my mother concerning a marriage proposal for Jane that came from one of her relatives who attended. He was a pilot in the Iran Imperial Air Force and, as such, was also a relative of the shah. Apart from the fact that we didn't even know him, my mother also mentioned that Jane was only thirteen. With respect, he said he would wait for marriage until she was fourteen. Returning the respect, Mother unyieldingly declined. I personally thought it was hilarious that Jane had been proposed to, but I guess as far as the adults were concerned, it was no laughing matter. Other than that, my day was pretty dull. I thought that being out of the van and on motionless land would be fun, but it was not. I decided to write in my journal.

Day Fifteen: April 22, 1975

Minah had given us some Iranian sweets as a gift. I wanted to eat the whole box, but Mother said we should wait until we leave. The old man tried to give me sugar and warm goats' milk again. Yuk! Jane got a marriage proposal. He he.

As usual, I had a bunch of questions, especially regarding the new religion we had encountered. Mother explained as much as she knew about the Muslim religion. It was brief but basically covered the five-times-a-day prayer call that I already had the unfortunate experience of hearing. She mentioned how men could have more than one wife. I asked about sultans and sheikhs, common words when mentioning mosques. She told me that they were wealthy men of important stature, who may have many wives called a harem, and if they did not want one of them anymore, all they had to say is "I divorce thee" three times in front of two witnesses, and they were divorced. There were other facts, but for some reason, these were the ones that made the biggest impression on me. It was all very intriguing. I wondered how she knew so much.

On the third morning, I woke up early. I trotted downstairs to the kitchen, somewhat fearful of approaching the old man, but I knew I was supposed to go there. When I entered the kitchen, he wasn't to be found. At first I was happy he was absent, and I thought I would just ignore my commands and take off, but then a picture of a glowering, red-faced Fiona entered my mind, and I thought better of it. I began to look around for him. I went to the ground floor and heard him outside with someone. It sounded like they were spraying water. I hoped that they were filling the pool for me to swim in, so I started running with anticipation out toward the driveway. When I turned to go toward the pool, I saw a river of blood being hosed down to the road. I looked over to the backyard and saw the lamb. It had been killed right there. I was in total shock. The old troll quickly handed the hose to the other man and hustled me back upstairs.

By then, everyone else was awake. I was crying, and all mayhem let loose. The old man was trying to explain in Farsi what had happened, and I was bawling to Mother about what they had done. It was awful. I knew he was a mean man, and I didn't like him. I was taken to the quarters and told that it was their way to make fresh food. The fluffy lamb had not been a pet but was actually dinner. I was devastated. I never wanted to see anything like that again. I made up my mind that I would never eat anything that was prepared at that house, whether it was vegetable or animal. So true was that, as we left that day. We said our good-byes to Fiona and thanked Minah for her hospitality. I had thought we were going to stay longer, but I think I caused too much chaos for Minah. My mother never did get to go to the mosque, and I felt bad because now she could not ask the Muslim god for a safe trip.

My mother did not appear to be unhappy with the situation. In fact, she was probably relieved that she could be in control again. Once on the road, everyone turned back to their usual selves. I was extremely glad, as that whole experience at Minah's house had been traumatic. Jane became a teenager again, and all was going well. We opened up the Iranian sweets that Minah had given us and ate the whole box. My mother justified eating all the candy at one time by telling us they all would have melted into one big lump in the heat and would have been ruined. It made sense to me.

At this point in the trip, we had to make it to Mashad. Faith had mentioned a large campsite there that was apparently a common spot for travelers to stay. We also heard about a few local hotels and hostels that were supposed to be quite comfortable. We were not absolutely sure what option we would go for, and we decided to wait until we arrived there before making a choice. Mashad was about four hundred and twenty-five miles from Tehran. Mother wanted to make it there that day, so it was back to musical chairs, with Ryan and her taking turns driving. We passed most of the higher elevations, and the terrain started to become more level, stretching out to foothills that led into a rocky desert.

Along the way, I began to see small, black, unidentified objects flitting across the road in a peculiar manner. Mother said she thought they were some sort of insect. At first she tried to dodge them, but it was quite impossible. We could almost feel the crunching as we drove over them. Eventually, we stopped briefly to see exactly what they were. It turned out they were dung beetles rolling large balls of animal poop this way and that. On further inspection, we saw that the busy critters were working furiously to get their balls of dung to their hole-in-the-ground hideouts. Quite unexpectedly, the beetles used their hind legs to push the oversize trophies about. They looked like they were in a cumbersome, backward-moving wheelbarrow race. It was quite fascinating and entertaining at the same time. Before I started asking all kinds of questions that only an entomologist could answer, we were back in the van, squishing the poor creatures under the tires again. We must have killed hundreds of them, but I figured that if they couldn't decide which side of the road they wanted to be on then they were kind of asking for it. Being completely naïve, I asked my mother why they were suicidal and wouldn't stop to let us pass before crossing the road. I don't recall a verbal response. Anyway, these beetles were a common occurrence for a hundred or so miles. By the time they started to whittle down, we had probably annihilated more than half the population. I was glad we were the only people driving out there, because all the tiny bugs might have perished had there been more traffic.

The roads now were more like well-worn grooves in the gravelly dessert. It might have been cemented over or had tarmac on it at one time, for all I knew, but at that point, there was not much of an actual road to speak of. Every few miles, we drove into a medium-size hole or over a boulder in the road, which in turn made everything in the van fall out of place, in particular the green bowl of sugar. The first time we went into a shallow pit, the tub came down right on top of my head. Jane thought it was hilarious, but it wasn't her head the tub fell on. I placed the tub back on top of the refrigerator, which had a circular indentation in which ice water was supposed to be poured. The depression was porous, so that the ice water could seep down and around the edges to keep the inside cold, but we never had any ice water, so the refrigerator was not used for cooling but for storage. The wok-shaped hollow, however, was the perfect size for the bowl of sugar to fit in, and that was why it was stored there. After the sugar bowl jumped out of position several times, we decided to have a warning signal to prepare me for the dangers of the dreaded Tupperware. "Bump" became the alert word. For miles, all Mother and Ryan said was "bump." I never understood why we didn't just put the stupid bowl somewhere else, but I didn't make the rules, so back on the refrigerator the bowl went, time and time again. The darn thing must have bounced off fifty times over a couple of hours! It occurred to me that the whole ordeal was designed to keep me occupied through the monotonous parts of the desert.

By midday, we were still completely alone in the middle of nowhere. We decided to take a short stop. Out came the shoes, cases, blankets, and such, and under the van they went. I had been wary of putting my stuff under the van after the stealing habits of the Turkish locals, so I just left my gear inside. While we were having lunch, we noticed that far off in the distance, on some foothills leading away from the mountains, there were camels walking along the horizon. We were so excited about seeing the animals walking out in the desert that Mother took out the camera to take pictures of them. She told me to stand in the frame so that it looked like something more than just a few camels on a hill. Later, when that film was developed, the picture looked like it was only of me, because the camels in the background appeared as tiny dots; so much for that photo. After the exhilarating sight of the camel specks, we finished lunch and took off. The heat was unbearable, and the road went on for miles and miles with no sign of civilization anywhere.

Around three in the afternoon, it started to get slightly breezy. We stopped the van and hopped out to assess the situation and to take a short tea break. When we went to unload the gear, we realized that we had left it under the van, possibly two hundred miles away. There was no way my mother was going back two hundred miles for a few pairs of shoes and blankets. Actually, I was not too upset about the situation, as I had not put my bags out to begin with. I guess the camels had been a distraction from the usual, enough for us to forget the gear. After the initial disappointment of losing property, Mother returned to her usual self, shrugging off the loss and continuing on with the navigational plans.

The weather had been changing, and the winds were picking up. In fact it was quite funny, because Mother had to take a potty break. She hid behind the van and did her thing, but every time she tried to use the toilet paper, it was lifted by the winds, and the sheets took to the air like mini kites. It was quite entertaining until Mother began screaming for help. I don't know what she thought anyone could do, but Ryan ran off behind the van, and a few minutes later, they both appeared relatively unharmed. Jane and I were sitting in our lawn chairs, playing cards and trying to hold back the laughter; in the end, we couldn't help it, and we both just let it all out. We thought Mother would be angry at us, but she too began to laugh.

After the stop and a quick assessment of the situation, we started on the road again, but Mother was clearly concerned about the unusual weather change. For me it was a relief, because it began to cool down dramatically. Up ahead in the distance, we saw the sky turning an ominous gray color. We were driving straight toward it, but in the middle of the desert there was nowhere to detour to escape the fast-approaching storm. We could go back, but either way, the darkness was gaining on us much faster than we could escape, and being chased by the quickly advancing storm and experiencing yet more setbacks was not on the agenda for the day. Mother was sure that we could bulldoze our way through the storm and come out a few minutes later on the other side unscathed, so we pressed on with enthusiasm. Before long, the worst downpour I had ever witnessed in my life began. There was thunder, lightning, and so much rain that within an hour it looked like we were out in the middle of the ocean. Every time lightning struck, the desert lit up, and there was an ethereal mirror effect on the fallen rain. All the clouds appeared as if they were on wet ground as the light reflected off the surface. It was an amazing sight but also rather daunting. As we drove on and on, we started passing a few people in vehicles that were stuck in huge muddy holes. We stopped by one vehicle that had four women wearing *abayas* and *burka* veils over their faces. Their vehicle was lodged in the ground, and we wanted to try to help them, but it was not long before we had also become trapped in the muddy water. It was also beginning to get really cold. For a country that had such hot days, I could not believe we were cold. It did not help that we had lost some of our blankets. The few people who were traveling on that road were now in the same predicament as we were. We were all stuck in the same area. No one could really do anything, as the water was at least three feet deep.

The rain started to seep in through the side doors, and I thought surely we were all going to drown if it didn't stop soon. My imagination started to kick in, and I wondered if this was going to be another forty days and forty night's ordeal; however, there was no ark in sight. Just when I thought that we were all going to die out there, we saw some large emergency tow trucks coming toward us. One by one, they towed everyone to safety in the nearest town. It turned out that we were not far away from our destination of Mashad. I could tell that a large amount of money came out of our funds for being towed out of the desert of water that night, as Mother had that look about her when she wrote down the expenses in the ledger. I wondered just how much worse this journey could get.

We woke up really early the next day. A mechanic told us that we needed to let the engine dry out for a few days before we tried to start up the van, so we set up at the camp in Mashad, fully aware that we would be there for a while. We were so preoccupied that morning with everything that was going on with the poor old drowned Dinosaur that we did not even notice until some hours later that there was a white Volkswagen van parked near some trees. We went over to see if it was Faith, Pat, and Keith. As we approached, we saw them hanging out with their cameras. Pat was focusing on some object when we came into his field of vision. He put down the camera and called to Faith and Keith. We had a group hug, and we were jumping around like kids. Well, I *was* one, but the adults were jumping around too! It was good times. Much of our time at the camp was spent with them. We parked really close together so we could make the two vehicles like a small clubhouse. It was fun for me, as it felt much like playing a game. Being at the Mashad camp was like a mini vacation, as we did not have to keep rushing off after every meal or every time we woke up.

At the Mashad camp, there were countless people from all over the world. We met a nice family with two daughters and a son. It was unclear where they were coming from, but I did know they were going across land to Canada. I was so happy that they had children, because it gave me a chance to be with people of my own age. The only problem was that one of the girls was very sick. She had been bitten by a dog and had contracted rabies. She had to stay in the camper and have injections every day. The other sister was too young, so I could not play her, either.

I was stuck with the older brother, who was one and a half years older than me and was quite an unsociable boy. Even though the couple was English, the son had a different name that I could not pronounce. He was mad at me because I said it incorrectly, and he told me that I was a stupid girl. I tried to tell him that I had another name that was hard to pronounce too, that my father had given me, but he did not believe me, and he told me I shouldn't tell lies to make someone else feel better.

After an afternoon with that miserable kid, I was ready to hang out with Jane again. She had made friends with a campground man who owned a bicycle that he let her ride. She rode up and let me sit on the back while she pedaled me around. At first, it was fun riding around camp as a passenger on the skinny bicycle—until I put my foot in the back spokes by accident and went tumbling over, right in front of Mr. Bad Attitude Boy. He had a good laugh at that, and I disliked him even more. My mother and Ryan had made good friends with his parents, so whether I liked it or not, I was stuck with having to play nice. This was extremely difficult, because no matter how hard I tried to be a fun companion, the kid would not have it.

The next day I experienced discomfort in my ankle due to the stupid bicycle wreck, so I decided I would not do anything that might injure me further. I was sitting along the roadside, drawing with a stick in the sand, when the ground started to rumble. At first I thought it was an earthquake, as it was quite a ground-shaking experience. I looked up to see the most massive bus I had ever seen in my life. It drove past and slowed to a grinding halt, with plumes of sand and dust shooting out from under the tires as it pulled up to the camp area. It stood unmoving and silent for about two minutes. It was curious, for sure. Suddenly and without any warning at all, the sides of the bus started to come down. Tables, chairs, and huge umbrellas were being put out on the parking lot. People were emerging, dressed all fancy, and taking seats at the tables. Waiters and cooks came out of the front of the bus and started serving lunch to the seated passengers. By now, the gigantic black bus had attracted the attention of my mother and other folks from the camp. Everyone just stared in amazement. This was, in fact, a German traveling hotel. It actually had floors with beds, toilets, showers, and catering. It was incredible. I wished that Mother had made it to the mosque to ask for one of these for us to travel in. After the patrons' lunch, they came down to mingle with the campers. They were really nice people, and I loved to hear them speak. The camp had an all-night party where everyone gathered around and shared their stories. It was an enjoyable evening. I felt safe and happy that we were hanging out with folks similar to us, and soon I forgot all the strife we had been through to get to this point in our trip.

I woke up later than usual the next morning. Mother, Jane, and Ryan were already doing their thing. They were going over to see the English family, and they told me that the son would be coming over to get me, and we were to go find the swimming pool on the other side of the camp and take a swim. Swim? I hadn't even known there was a pool, so I eagerly awaited the arrival of Mr. Miserable. He finally strolled up to the van and gestured for me to follow him. I thought that maybe we could try to make friends again. I tried to make polite conversation, but he was not interested. I asked how old he was, and he told me he was twelve. Just because I had heard different and not to be rude, I told him that I thought his parents had said he was eleven and a half. He was mad at me again, and he told me that eleven and a half was almost twelve, so what was the difference? I told him six months, and he became more agitated with me. I told him that I was ten and not nine. He just shook his head and said something under his breath that sounded like "idiot." With that, we arrived at the pool, which was empty. Mr. Miserable Boy gave me an angry glare and strutted off like it was my fault that the pool had no water in it. He clearly was an unhappy child, and I felt bad for him. I knew there was nothing I could say to make him feel better, so I just followed him back to our camp area. When we reached our parents, he slid into their luxury van and disappeared. I didn't see him again, as they were going to be on their way that day in the opposite direction from us. It made me sad, really, because even though he was so unhappy and seemingly mad at me all the time, he was the only other kid around, and I actually thought we could have been pals, but I guessed that wasn't going to happen.

After my mother and Ryan said good-bye to their English buddies, we went back to our side of camp. It was a doubly sad day for me, because not only did the English family leave, but Faith and company were also leaving. They had stayed an extra day, but they said they really had to get a move on. We hugged them all and said our farewells. Faith noticed I was upset. She kneeled down to face level and told me not to be sad, as we would meet again sometime. I hoped we would. Again I waved good-bye to them as they drove onto the dusty road. I felt like I was going to cry, but as they were driving off, another couple we had met in Turkey drove into camp. The Sothebys had arrived.

It was so good to see them again. I kind of wished that they had arrived a few days before, so we all could have been together with Faith. Still, it was great that they had arrived while we were still there. They stayed the night at the camp, and we spent that evening conversing with them. We talked about where we were traveling and how long we would stay at each place. They were taking almost the same route as we were up to India, at least to Delhi, and then we would go our separate ways. Just in case we did not meet up with them along the way, we exchanged contact addresses, so that we might write to each other, or even meet up again after our trips. It was nice to know such interesting people, and even though time spent with other travelers was short-lived, every encounter we had was incredibly special, for most of the trip time we spent alone and isolated from anyone else.

The next day, the Sothebys had already taken off by the time I woke up. By now, it was time to start getting back on track ourselves and continue on our way to Afghanistan. We had been in Mashad for six days, relaxing and taking it easy. It was a welcome rest, but life goes on, and we had a destination to reach. The van had dried out thoroughly by now in the scorching heat, and after some tinkering in the back of the old jalopy, the engine roared as if eager itself to move on. Mother wanted to spend one more day in Mashad, but in a motel so we could get proper showers and rest in comfortable beds before the long drive.

We drove about thirty miles out from Mashad before we came upon a motel in the middle of nowhere. Apparently, it was the last one before reaching Afghanistan, so we were advised to stay there. We booked in, had a nap, woke up, and went downstairs to have something to eat. Soon after we finished our meal, two men came over and befriended us. They said they were visiting from Afghanistan and appeared extremely interested in our travel arrangements. They laughed and joked around and appeared to be generally nice people. The restaurant side of the motel began to close, so the gentlemen invited us up to their room to continue the conversation. Like so many grown-ups we had met, they seemed ultra-cool, because they didn't mind that Jane and I were there, and they always included us in the conversation. It made me feel very mature.

When we were in their room, they offered Mother and Ryan a drink of ice-cold beer from bottles. Ryan accepted, and Mother declined. They were Muslims and didn't drink. I had no idea where they produced the beer from, or why, but I didn't spend too much time thinking about it either. Once Ryan had opened his beer, they started talking again. This time, one of the men put a lump of dirt on the table. He looked at my mother and asked if she knew what it was. With a confused look on her face, she observed the brown sand rock and said she thought it looked like dried mud. Ryan interjected, saying it was hashish. Indeed, that was what it was. Jane leaned over and whispered in my ear that hashish was illegal contraband that the border patrol would look for. The men asked if my mother or Ryan would like to buy some, but after they declined, the men said they wanted them to stash a whole bunch of drugs in the sides of the van to transport over the border to Afghanistan. I am not certain whether they had exchanged hashish for some other illegal drug in Iran, or if they wanted to us to take hashish to Afghanistan to trade for something else. Whatever the case, the men said they would pay a good price for the transportation once we arrived safely on the other side in a village in the province of Herat. They guaranteed Mother that we had nothing to worry about and that they would be following right behind us the whole way. They said they had picked us because we were an innocent family, and no one at the Afghanistan border would suspect English folk with children of transporting drugs.

My mother kept her calm the whole time, shook their hands, and said we would meet them promptly at six in the morning to arrange the filling of the van with the contraband. Jane and I looked at each other in disbelief, but my mother gave us a calm nod of assurance, and we proceeded back to our room. Once inside our room, she shut the door tightly, placing her back up against it as if to keep people out, and whispered so she would not be overheard. She told us that we should get packing now, because we were leaving promptly at three in the morning. She wanted enough time to pass for the men to fall asleep. We would then slip out the side door and into the van to escape, as she had no intention of sneaking drugs in our van. She looked scared, but as usual, she was handling the situation.

None of us could sleep, in anticipation of our departure. Ryan had been taking some of our belongings to the van every now and again, trying not to cause suspicion. At three in the morning, Ryan went to get the van ready for departure. He pushed it a few feet away from the motel so we didn't wake anyone up with the sound of our noisy engine. We went downstairs and waited silently in the side entrance for him to signal. He waved us on, and we ran to the van as quickly as possible. Mother shot into the driver's seat, and Ryan pushed the van a few more feet and then jumped in. Mother started it up, put the headlights on, and began driving as fast as she could toward Afghanistan and away from the motel.

We were not even one minute down the road when we saw a jeep leaving the motel. It was them. They must have heard us start the van, because they were now in pursuit. We thought we had managed to evade them, but they were gaining on us. Mother floored the accelerator, and the Dinosaur began to roar across the desert road as fast as it could. The van was being pounded by small rocks and gravel that bounced furiously off the sides, making a horrible sound as if we were being shot by pellets. Because of the dust, we could barely see whether or not the dealers were on our tail. Every now and again, the dust cleared, and Mother saw in her side mirrors that they were behind us in the distance. Eventually, their headlights grew smaller and smaller. After about thirty minutes, they finally turned around and went back the other way. We all felt immediate relief. I was still shaking in my shoes, though. I think we all were. Even though the men were clearly out of sight, Mother kept on driving non-stop until we reached Afghanistan.

I was beginning to realize that, no matter what, this wasn't going to be an easy trip. When my mother had spoken of adventure and excitement, I definitely had not imagined any of the situations we had encountered so far. I believed we would be having a great time, possibly swimming in the ocean, taking short walks along beaches, viewing all the wonders of the world, and basically having a safe and enjoyable time. I knew it was not supposed to be a vacation, but I didn't expect mayhem and cataclysm around every corner. So far it was feeling more and more like a nightmare that worsened every time I went to sleep. I began thinking that Ryan's idea of returning to England was a good one, but then again, we would have to pass all the difficulties going back. It was a really trying time for me, not knowing what would happen next. Mother appeared to be handling everything fairly well, like this sort of thing happened every day. The drug dealers had crawled under my skin, though, and left a really uncomfortable feeling. The only redeeming factor was that we were only two countries away from India. I thought about it for a while and figured that only two options existed between here and India. We either lived or died. Everything in between was already happening.

It was around noon by the time we arrived at the Afghanistan border. It was already unbelievably hot. The sun was blazing, baking the ground until it cracked. Just a few days before, we had been freezing our behinds off in a desert storm, and now we were sweltering. Along with trying to cope with the heat, Jane and I were still pretty shaken up by the drug traffickers and were still wary of them, even though we were pretty much on safe ground now. It was not a comfortable time, but at least we were making progress. We went through the Iran side of the border and drove up to the Afghanistan side, where we would do the usual checking in. When we pulled up, a large man who looked like a general came out with his men, looking more like militia than border patrol. He looked the van up and down and looked at all of us. We were all standing near the van, waiting for Mother to get her papers, passports, and visas ready for inspection. When she had the papers in order, she went to the general to show him that we had all the requirements to enter the country. Before she could say a word, the general asked to search the van. My mother looked hurt and frustrated at first, because we had just been through hell so we would not break the law, but then she refused indignantly, explaining that we were just travelers and all we needed to do was drive through Afghanistan to get to Pakistan. Her attitude did not impress the general, and again he asked to search the van. Wearily, Mother's shoulders curled inward, and her head tilted forward in a defeated manner. She looked down and shook her head; once again we faced complications. We had been through so much already, and quite frankly, unloading and reloading the van was a hassle, especially in the searing heat.

While her head was down, Mother noticed that we had parked next to an anthill and that the occupants were scurrying all over the place. Now, these were no ordinary ants. They were huge, the size of bath spiders, one to one and a half inches long. She started screaming and stepping on them as they scrambled across her feet and tried to climb up her legs. It would have been funny, but the general went into a rage. He told her to stop stomping on his country's ants, saying that she had no right to come to Afghanistan and kill his people's insects. His voice was booming as he spoke the words with his Afghan accent. It was a truly unexpected and terrifying moment that made me gasp and almost jump out of my skin. He told Mother that he would pull the van into pieces if she did not comply. She retorted by telling him that if his men pulled it apart, they would be the ones who put it back together. He was so angry that he just turned away and marched back into his office. Mother was on her last thread of sanity by then. Other travelers were looking over at us, wondering what the commotion was about. Most hopped into their vehicles and drove away quickly, so they wouldn't get involved.

The temperature outside was 120° Fahrenheit, and it was not much better in the shade. The heat was getting to everyone, and the situation was no better. We just stood around, waiting to see what Mother was going to do. Ryan just lingered near the van with a stunned look on his face. He was not as bullheaded as Mother, so he was not about to intervene. While she was contemplating the next step, we heard a whistle. With that, all the border guards lined up outside the building in two long rows, facing each other. It was time for the daily guard inspection. The two rows of men were armed and standing at attention. Noticing that the general was completely ignoring our needs, Mother dashed forward, pushing away at the guards. She strutted down a long hallway that led to his office. Ryan, Jane, and I followed like a bunch of lemmings. Mother stood in front of the general, who was now seated behind his huge wooden desk, and demanded that he let us pass. She threw the papers on the desk and ordered him to stamp the paperwork and let us through without incident. He just sat there silently, shoulders pinned back, staring at us. Beads of sweat trickled down the sides of his face from the black hair he tried to conceal under his cap. I am sure that her frenzied conduct took him by surprise, and with a noticeably flushed face, he looked over the paperwork. His body did not move, only his eyes as they darted over the documents. We just stood there like a group of reprimanded schoolgirls in front of the headmaster, waiting to hear the final punishment. Finally, he spoke.

"No, Mrs. English, you may not enter my country," he said, staring menacingly into her eyes.

Mother demanded an explanation, other than the fact that we had refused to let him search the van, and that she had caused mass murder of his ants. He told us that the vehicle pass had expired one day ago, and we would have to go back to Iran to get it renewed. Mother snatched the paperwork back and glanced at it. We could tell from the look on her face that he was telling the truth. She strutted back through the hallway and outside, pushing past the guards again, and leaped back in the van. We drove back over to the Iran side and stopped along the road. Mother cried for a while and then regained her composure. She said she felt embarrassed because some Australian lads we had met previously were at that border and had witnessed the scene. We all assured her it wasn't a big deal, because it really was hot, and all our brains were frying. Of all the details that could have upset her about that incident, it was the Australians seeing her in a rage that upset her the most.

We sat there between borders for a while, trying to reexamine the situation. I knew that whatever Mother decided, we would have to drive in Iran again. My first concern was the possibility that we would bump into the drug traffickers again. Plus a new concern entered my mind. It was the dung beetles. I hoped that no one in Iran saw us drive over the millions of beetles that we had, because if this general was that angry at Mother for killing maybe thirty ants, then I couldn't imagine what the punishment would be for almost causing beetle genocide. It was extreme thinking, but I realized that anything was possible out here.

Mother contemplated every route we could take to Pakistan, but it always ended up with us having to go back to Mashad and pass the motel, no matter what. It appeared that there was no practical way to Pakistan except through Afghanistan. Mother had also inadvertently forgotten to pay the motel during all the commotion of escape, which made going back there so much harder. The only place we could get another vehicle pass was Mashad. There was no alternative. So with brave faces, we started back on the over two-hundred-mile trek back to Mashad. Every time I saw a vehicle coming toward us, I thought that it might the jeep men. I could not relax, nap, draw, or write anything, knowing that those men could find us. When we arrived back at the motel, the owners had not even realized that we had checked out for the day. The jeep was gone, so Mother just walked in, paid the motel people, and left. We went on to Mashad, where we received a new vehicle pass for one month, just like that. We found a hotel to stay in and crashed. We didn't wake up until the next day.

It was mid-morning by the time we were all up and about. We must have caught up on some much-needed sleep. We had breakfast at the hotel, gathered up our belongings, and set off once again to the Afghanistan border. It was really quiet the whole way there, and Mother had an unusual calm about her. We were all a bit concerned about how she was going to deal with the general today. When we arrived at the border, the afternoon guard inspection was beginning. We pulled up, exited the van, and proceeded to the office, Mother in the lead. This time, the guards were lined up inside the building, against the walls of the long hallway leading to the general. We walked quietly and calmly past them and entered the office. The general was sitting behind his desk, shoulders back, his facial expression as tight as a corset, and like the day before, he just stared at us. My mother had instructed us all to look pleasant and smile. She stepped forward.

"General," she said, "I am so sorry for my behavior yesterday and for killing your ants, but I am just a simple Englishwoman who is not used to your country's fine, hot weather and your lovely insects. I would like to see your wonderful country and show respect to you and your people." She paused. "I have been to Mashad and have the required paperwork that you need for my vehicle. If your men wish to search the van, you are welcome to let them begin." She smiled nicely, lowered her eyes, and made a slight nod toward him.

He gestured for her to show him the paperwork she was holding. Mother graciously placed the appropriate papers in front of him. It was dead silent in that room, except for a slight tapping noise coming from the lone ceiling fan. My spindly legs were shaking, and I thought I was going to pee in my pants. After a few minutes of watching the general glance over the paperwork that he had covered his desk with, he looked up. He inhaled a deep breath of air and let it out really slowly. Then he spoke.

"You know, you maker me so angry yesterday, I shev my head." He spoke loudly but calmly.

I wondered what in the blazers he was talking about, but an explanation was close at hand. He pulled off his hat and pointed to his shiny, bald scalp. I don't know about the others, but I almost laughed, cried, and urinated at the same time. My nerves were getting the better of me, but I stayed quiet. My mother, on the other hand, had something she wanted to say to him.

"You know who you look like?" she asked with a big smile.

I felt myself jump slightly when she spoke these familiar words. I diverted my eyes from the huge general to look at my mother. I was hoping that she would be able to read the "I don't think this is a good time" look on my face, but she didn't see me. She was still looking at the general with a fixed smile on her face. I wasn't certain that I wanted to hear his response. He stared at her with an inquisitive frown. In the end, she gave up waiting for an answer.

"You look like Telly Savalas, big American film star," she said with an emphasis on the word "big." She even made huge, circular arm movements to show just how big Telly Savalas was.

The general nodded slowly as though recalling the name, and then he smiled.

"Yes," he said. "I know this Kojak, American film star," he said with a more casual air about him.

He had the biggest smile on his face you can imagine. He actually did look like Telly Savalas, unlike the Steve McQueen character in France. I had seen enough episodes of *Kojak* to know that.

He picked up his stamp and plunged it down on the passport, handed back the pile of papers, and shook Mother's hand. He told us that there was no need for a vehicle search and wished us a pleasant trip through his country. Once again, Mother had made good with one of her crazy actor speeches. I couldn't believe it. I had hoped that she would not do that again, but it worked. Now there was another very happy actor lookalike running around, and they were both border patrol officials that had encountered my mother.

Chapter 8

Afghanistan

We all let out huge sighs of relief as we drove away from the ludicrous border situation. I didn't even want to look at the stamp in the passport. I couldn't care less what it looked like; I was just thankful we had it. It appeared that we were not going to escape the unexpected, no matter what. It was evident that even a well-organized plan could go awry. I couldn't understand how something so simple as driving to Australia could have so many upheavals. I kept on thinking how easy it would be just to find an airport and fly straight to Australia, but I knew that was not going to happen. We just had to trudge onward.

The drive through the province of Herat was pretty straightforward, although I kept looking behind us just in case that jeep was somewhere out on the rocky road, ready to jump out of nowhere and chase us down. About two hours after crossing the border, we stopped at a small village to get water and provisions. The whole time, we were overly aware of the surroundings, as the situation had made us extremely paranoid. Even though we had not actually been threatened with harm if we did not comply with the drug traffickers' demands, there was still a feeling of impending doom if we did not get away from Afghanistan in a hurry. The worst feeling was when the locals stared at us. It was not unusual for local inhabitants to be curious about travelers, and for the most part, we were used to it; but now it was different, because we didn't know if they knew who we were. Maybe this was the village we were supposed to meet the smugglers at. Apart from a few curious residents, and concerns over a slowly deflating tire, everything went well, fortunately. We soon left, but every time we passed a village or farm hut, I wondered if the dreaded jeep would soon be tailing us. We drove to the city of Herat with nobody behind us. In fact, it was really weird, because there were very few people at all driving on those desert roads. I felt really afraid and defenseless, even though I had my family with me.

The city of Herat was big and well populated. Our feeling of vulnerability began dissipating as the city people welcomed us to their country. While we shopped for provisions, everyone was helpful, and they seemed not to hold any grudges toward tourists. The haggling tradesmen were funny. I found it strange that you couldn't just buy something for the listed price. The merchants would be offended if you didn't try to get a better deal. It was a kind of game. If you didn't know the rules, it could mean trouble. Mother caught on well, and before long, she was haggling left, right, and center.

We had run out of water purification tablets, so from here on, we had to buy bottled water, which was nearly impossible. The other option was to buy bottled drinks, such as canned fruit juice, if you could find it, or soda. We couldn't have any fresh juice, due to the condition of our refrigerator. Occasionally expensive green bottles of sparkling Perrier would be available for purchase, but Mother didn't want to overspend on water, especially if it sparkled. Tea would not brew the same, even with the fizz boiled out of it. Eventually we found a place that sold a generic brand of bottled water and stocked up. I am sure Mother's bartering skills worked wonders for that, as the shop owner gave me a gift. At first, Mother told me that I shouldn't take it, but the man insisted it was free and that I could have it. He handed me a small brass camel. I was overjoyed to receive a present from someone, especially as it was a really nice, shiny camel. At first I thought it was solid gold; the merchant laughed when I asked him if it was. Still, gold or not, I really appreciated the gift, and I was extremely pleased with my new possession. After the trading was over, the merchant asked us to visit later at his home and have dinner with him. Even though the man was gracious and kind, Mother respectfully declined the invitation, because as usual, we were in a hurry. He wished us a happy trip, and we went on our way.

This city was quite unusual. Unlike the cities in Turkey, which had remnants of many different cultures, Herat had its own unique attributes. In the early evening when the sun was going down, the city looked pink. If you caught the sunset at just the right moment, you could see the heat from the day shimmering up from the dusty streets, surrounding the coral buildings in a vaporous glow. It looked quite amazing, considering the city streets were actually anything but glamorous. Animals ran freely in the road, and now and then a dog or cat would come out and begin eating a fly-ridden corpse of another animal that had perished.

The dogs and cats looked different here, too. They were skinny, their bones stuck out, and they had no fur except for a few scraggly hairs sticking up in different directions, like a cactus. Mother told me that animals didn't need fur in hot countries. It made sense, plus very few animals were kept as pets, so they were not fed well; that was why they were so thin. Many of the animals were rabid, and no one would take one in, for fear of catching the dreaded disease. It was incredibly sad for me to see, because I liked and appreciated animals. This was one of the many things that were different about countries of the Middle East, things that had a deep emotional impact on me.

Apart from the sadness of the suffering animals, I did observe other attributes of the city that were of interest to me. The most incredible mosque caught my eye, and it was actually blue on the outside. It had hundreds of pairs of shoes stacked up around it. Not everyone in Herat was Muslim, but judging by the shoes, many were. There was something intriguing about so many dedicated Muslims. If they did not make it to a mosque in time for prayer, apparently they rolled out a mat, no matter where they were, and prayed. That is how I saw it, anyway.

So far, Afghanistan was not as bewildering or frightening as I had thought it was going to be. I don't know if that was because I was adapting to the many unexpected changes, or if this place was just safer. The chaotic circumstances stayed pretty constant through the last few countries, and as long as a new situation did not make a dramatic change, I felt I could handle anything that might occur. But we still had almost five hundred miles of Afghanistan to cover before we got to the Pakistan border, so I knew not to get too comfortable with the idea that nothing else could go wrong.

Looking back on the day, I remembered the hospitality of the people, including the man who gave me the token of friendship. That evening, I took a good look at the camel. It stood with a slight tilt. Any small movement made the camel tumble over, making a noisy clanking sound. Regardless of that problem, I liked it and considered the camel a lucky charm. I decided it was a male, even though there were no distinguishing features to determine this, and I called him Camel Merlin after the wizard from the many tales of King Arthur. I hoped he would bring us some magical luck.

I don't remember falling asleep, but at some time during the evening drive away from the great city of Herat, I must have dropped off. I woke up to find that I was alone in the van. It was dark outside, and I could hear people talking. I looked out of the window and saw my mother, Jane, and Ryan standing outside huddled together as they talked to some men who were carrying flashlights and oil lamps. Apparently, the conversation was at its end, as my family jumped in the van, and we took off in a hurry. I asked why they had stopped, but all I was told was that there had been an accident on the road involving a large truck. As we drove away, I looked back and saw the men surrounding a huge truck that was sprawled across the street. Mother, Ryan, and Jane were looking forward and didn't appear to be interested in the commotion. I was glad it was not us in the wreck, and I held Camel Merlin in my hand, thanking him for bringing us some much-needed luck.

After spending the night at a motel, we set out on our way to Kandahar. The plan was to pass through Kandahar and then cross the Afghanistan/Pakistan border to Quetta. It was going to be a long drive—four hundred miles, give or take a few—and it would take us into higher elevations again. It had been desert for the last few hundred miles, but now we were going back into the all-too-familiar mountainous terrain. We were told that nomadic tribes lived scattered throughout the mountains, and that they kept to themselves, as long as no trouble was instigated. The last thing we wanted was any more trouble.

At first, we didn't see anyone or anything for miles, which was becoming common, but then out of the blue, we spotted three men on horses on top of a hilly part of the mountain range. They had black wraps draped around their heads and shoulders and were heavily armed with what I can only describe as very large bullets strapped across their bodies. As we drove past them, they just watched us. They didn't move or ride toward us. They just stared, and their horses were as still as statues. After a few minutes, we looked back, and they were gone, just like that. Similar groups appeared along the way, but no one confronted us. I was so grateful for that.

That day, we reached a small community that was on a plain between the mountains. Mother decided it was time to take a rest. She had been driving for hours and needed to take a break. After we set up the van for our usual lunch and tea, some barefoot children came over to see us. They were all laughing and playing around us. Mother gave some sweets to the children, and they were ecstatic. They acted like they had never seen candy before. They didn't even open it to eat until Mother showed them how. They were overjoyed and ran off to tell others about the whole event. About thirty minutes later, we were beginning to pack up to get back on the road when a young girl came up to the van by herself and started talking quietly to us. We couldn't understand her, but we assumed she had come for some treats. The candy had all been given away. Mother felt so bad that we had nothing to give her. Suddenly I remembered that I had hidden away the box of rose guest soaps before we left, and quickly I grabbed them out of the hiding spot to show Mother. Relieved that we had something to give the girl, Mother opened the box and took out one of the roses, put some water on it, and started to lather it up in her hands. The girl sat watching with wide eyes. Mother put out her hands to show the girl that it was for washing your hands and smelled really good. She made sure that the girl didn't think they were to eat. After the demonstration, Mother took out the two other soaps and handed them to her. The girl put them to her nose and smelled the rosy aroma. She was smiling like it was Christmas. She cradled the soaps in her hands and then wrapped them up in a small piece of cloth and hid it in a scarf-like belt that hung around her waist. She nodded to us in thanks and ran off to her home, smiling and skipping the whole way.

It was thought-provoking that such small tokens made the children so happy. Mother had thought that the soaps were useless and would serve no purpose, but they brought joy to a small Afghan girl. I was glad I had decided to sneak them on board. It made me sad to think about the way the kids here lived. They were living in terrible conditions, with rancid water that was pumped from the ground and one hole-in-the-ground toilet, if they were lucky, that all the villagers had to use. They lived in mediocre shacks, and sometimes there were not even any brick buildings at all, but this was their lifestyle, and they were used to it.

As we set off down the road, I looked over the few toys and belongings that Mother had let me bring. I was thankful for my playthings and hoped I would never have to be without them. One toy that was special to me was a mouse that my grandmother had given me. She had bought it during her last visit to Australia. I was attached to all my toys, but this one had special meaning, as I felt like we were taking him back home. He was a cute thing called Wumsey with a gray and white body, huge eyes, and big, fluffy, pink ears. Fixed on his paw was a lone daisy with crisp white petals and a huge yellow middle. Pasted to his face was a petite felt smile that made me feel content, especially after many of the insane situations we had been experiencing. I felt somewhat silly finding comfort in a toy, especially as I was nine, but nevertheless I took advantage of anything that made me feel positive during these strange days. I hoped that soon we would be returning Wumsey to his homeland, mainly because that was where I wanted to be. Even though we were almost to India, we still had many, many miles to go. It felt like we were never going to get there.

A few hundred miles down the road from the village, we stopped for another break. We were not far from Kandahar. It was the next city on our steppingstone list, and I couldn't wait to get there. It meant we were nearing the end of the road trip. The whole journey so far had been different and somewhat exciting, but I couldn't wait for it to be over. We were almost out of range of the really high mountains, which I was always happy about. I feared the mountains more than anything else, because of the condition of the roads, the height from which we could fall, and the rockslides. I really just wanted to keep moving, but I knew we needed to stop, because driving long distances always made Mother tired. I accepted that I had no control of the travel matters and hopped out of the van.

As was frequently the case, I could not see any villages, towns, farm huts, or nomadic tribes in any direction. There was always a disquieting feeling when we were in remote desert areas. I imagined that we were on another planet much of the time, but Mother was always confident that everything was as it was supposed to be. Before we settled in for tea, Mother inspected the van and checked the oil, engine, radiator, and other things like that, and then the outside of the van, particularly the tires. She noticed a couple of dings in the old green paint from when we had shot across the desert in Iran, but she said they were only cosmetic damage and not really a major concern. We had already talked about painting the van all psychedelic once we lived in Perth, so dings were the least of our problems.

Once satisfied that everything was fine, we began our regular routine. Belongings were placed up against the side of the van now, a precaution we had started taking so we would not leave our stuff under the vehicle again. Out came the stove, kettle, cups, the usual. I sat next to the van and looked at Camel Merlin while the tea was being made. Mother handed me my cup, but it was not sweet enough, so I asked her for more sugar, as we had plenty. That sugar bowl was like a magic sugar bowl from hell. It always fell on my head and never seemed to get lighter. Anyhow, my mother refused to put more sugar in my tea and told me it was enough. She told me that it was the same amount that she always used. I was no fool, though. I could tell it was not the same, and I argued with her. I was more upset that she thought I couldn't tell than I was that she refused to put more in. For whatever reason, I was in a terrible mood. With Camel Merlin in my hand, I started walking off into the dry, hot desert.

"Where do you think you're going?" Mother blurted out from the van.

"I am going away," I retorted, not even looking back.

"Well, we're leaving soon, so you better start coming back now," she said, somewhat flustered.

I ignored her and continued walking toward nowhere. I could see some rocky hills up ahead, and I assumed that there would be a village, or maybe a wealthy sheikh that looked like Omar Sharif living in a huge, black, air-conditioned tent with everything inside that one would need to live a comfortable life in the desert. I imagined his harem all dressed up in beautiful, flowing dresses and sheer veils that showed only their eyes, with perhaps a glimpse of their faces through the translucent cloth. One day, I could grow up and be one of those women, I thought; I could deal with that. If I couldn't make it there on foot, I would just wait until the sheikh's servants came with camels, and I would ride on camelback to the magical tent, or maybe Camel Merlin would change into a real camel and take me away. All of these irrational thoughts were popping into my head as I boldly stepped where no English girl had stepped before. Apparently, Mother was not the only person who was affected by the hot Afghanistan heat. In the background, I heard Ryan, Mother, and Jane calling for me to come back.

"We're leaving now!" they all called. They paused and then started again. "Really, we are going now!" they shouted.

I ignored them, knowing full well that they would not leave me in the middle of the desert in Afghanistan. Then I heard the engine start up and the wheels speed away up the rocky road. I turned and saw them driving off without me, sand and dust flying up from the tires. I felt a sudden wave of fear and ran after them as fast as I could.

"Wait for me!" I screamed while running as fast as my skinny legs would take me.

My legs hurt so much, probably because my muscles were suffering from atrophy due to limited exercise. I took off so fast that I couldn't run any more after only a few seconds. Finally, the van stopped.

"Are you coming or not?" my mother roared at me.

"Yes, yes, I am coming," I said.

When I finally clambered into the van, Jane had a stupid grin on her face. It seemed to say, "You're an idiot. What did you expect?"

After that day of momentary insanity, especially the part about being in a harem, I never moved too far away from the van again, and I didn't refuse a cup of tea, sugar or no sugar. I cuddled up to Wumsey the mouse and fell asleep.

When I came around, we were stopped at another small village, a few miles away from Kandahar. I really needed to go to the bathroom and, seeing as we were already stopped, needed to find a toilet as opposed to using the tin. I hopped out of the van to find Mother and Ryan talking to a couple of guys. They looked like the Australians who had driven away at high speed at the Iran/Afghanistan border. I had to disturb her conversation so she could take me to the local toilet, but she was so engrossed that she just pointed the way to a hut near a field, which for the past few countries had been pretty much normal for a public toilet. It was similar to the water pump, in that the whole village used this one hut. One village, one bathroom hut, and one water pump: that was normal here.

I ran into the wooden hut and was just about to crouch over the ceramic hole in the floor when a huge lizard leaped over my shoulder and out in front of me. I almost fell in the dirty hole, and I let out a horrified scream. Not knowing what was wrong, my mother ran over in a panic. When she saw it was a lizard, she just chuckled. I was quite traumatized by the huge reptile, but as usual, Mother blew it off as being nothing. Worse than the lizard, though, was the fact that this hole-in-the-ground toilet didn't even have water or a jug available for use, like several of the others before. Toilet paper was not the thing here. Fortunately, being prepared as usual, Mother had tissues on her, so I was saved. How I yearned to sit on a proper throne and have rolls and rolls of toilet paper to use. Instead, I had to deal with stinky holes in the ground decorated with excrement for wallpaper. It was gross.

Once I had finished in the hut, I came out to see Mother and Ryan still talking with the guys. Like so many others, they were traveling around the Middle East and Asia. They were called Rob and Phil. We had met them before briefly, but we only learned their names now. Like Faith and Pat, Rob and Phil were traveling while filming and taking pictures of everything they saw. I wished we had brought a better camera and lots of film. I had made so many observations that I would like to have photographs of, to put with the journal that I had been neglecting recently. It did occur to me that one day we might meet up with some of the people we had made friends with, and I could get copies of the photographs they had taken while we were together.

Initially, Rob and Phil were traveling on the same route to Pakistan as we were, but they had changed their minds. From Kandahar they were going to Kabul. Rob had been discussing the nomadic people and bandits associated with said tribes. He told us horrific stories about European travelers being robbed or murdered, especially in no man's land and Quetta. They had been advised to go another way, past Kabul and on to a mountain route called the Khyber Pass, and then to the Afghanistan/Pakistan border, as Quetta, they had been told, was extremely dangerous.

Rob told us a story about two travelers who had been murdered in the mountains going to Quetta. He said that two young men and a woman had camped in their sleeping bags outside their vehicle, due to the heat. The girl slept in the middle and had a guy on each side of her. When she woke up in the morning, she noticed that they had switched positions in the night and wondered why they had made the change. On further inspection, she realized that while she had slept, someone had cut off her friends' heads and swapped them. There was no good part to that story, except that it happened several months ago. I was relieved, as I didn't want those victims to be Faith and her friends.

After hearing of the potential dangers, my mother thought it would be a better idea to take the northern route to Kabul. It was neat to have some other people to drive along with us again, as we had not seen any of the other crew since Iran. Everyone agreed that we should try to make it to Kabul and then to the Khyber Pass that day and before nightfall. We still had at least another two hundred miles to travel before we arrived in Kabul, so without further discussion, we packed ourselves in the vehicles and made our way to the next destination. By the time we all arrived there, it was pretty late, so we all stayed in a motel for the night and decided to drive the Khyber Pass the following day.

The next morning, we went to the parking lot, where Rob and Phil were already tinkering with their cameras and such. As soon as we piled into the van, it was time to go. Rob and Phil were anxious to get to Pakistan that day, which was very probable, as it was only about one hundred and fifty miles to the border. So off we set again. I always felt more secure when we had company on the road, even if we were in different vehicles. It was fun, like a race of sorts. On the way, Mother and Rob took turns being the leader. Rob's vehicle had the capacity to take off quickly and keep on going, so I was certain that they just let us believe we were ahead some of the time. Still, the old Dinosaur kept up, and we had a moment of entertainment while pretend racing.

About an hour or so later, we stopped in the city of Jalalabad. While we had lunch, there was a discussion about the mountainous trek along the Khyber Pass. I didn't understand why this pass through the mountains would be any more treacherous than the previous ones we had driven on, but apparently it was enough to cause concern. I started to get a little apprehensive about this Khyber Pass, but I knew better than to say anything about it, like, "Hey, let's not go that way!" The Khyber was supposed to be less dangerous than Quetta, but from the talk, it sounded to me like it was just as bad. Fortunately it was only about thirty miles to the other side. I wondered how hard that could be. Mother could do thirty miles in thirty minutes if she wanted to.

We left Jalalabad with Rob and Phil following behind, and we made it to the Afghanistan/Pakistan border with relative ease. The guys went through to the Pakistan side pretty quickly and said they would wait for us. After we had our passports stamped and papers approved, we drove through to Pakistan. Rob and Phil had already done their money trading and provisions check and were ready to go. As we still had our business to take care of, we said our good-byes and parted ways. I was saddened yet again that we had to go it alone, but at least we'd had company for a while. Plus I figured we would probably catch up with them somewhere in Pakistan. The last thing they advised was not to wait too long to get on the Pass.

Seeing as they had already left, Mother decided to park at the border for a while. We would rest and get our provisions taken care of without a rush. We parked the van near the side of a large hill, put a few bulky items by the van, and started to make tea. I also took out my all-important blue tin, which was clean, and placed it under the van. This was one item that was understandably still required to be set out under the van during parking times. While Ryan stayed inside the van looking over the map, Mother, Jane, and I went off to change currency.

Hearing a weird clanking noise, I looked back to see a man running up the hill with my Porta-Potty. I grabbed Mother and yelled at her to get my tin back. By then, Ryan was emerging from the van with the usual perplexed look on his face. The thief disappeared over the hill within seconds. While explaining to Ryan what happened, we started to put all our belongings back in the van, having decided to have tea later. I was so mad; of all things, my pee pot had been swiped. Mother made me feel better by telling me not to worry, as he would get what was coming to him once he stored his *chapatis* in there. It was a nasty thought, but I did have a chuckle, and before long, the loss was almost forgotten. We locked up the van and went off together to find someone to exchange currency with.

At this border, numerous tribesmen were walking around, making deals on currency exchange. There was no real bank to speak of, and we had to hope we chose an honest man to change money with. While Mother and Ryan were off trying to find a good deal, Jane and I wandered off to find our own deal. Jane had some cash and the bag of English pennies, which she was going to try to exchange with someone. We were told that no one would change the pennies, but any notes would be considered. We found a guy willing to change the note. Jane asked me to place the money in my shoe, as we didn't have a wallet or purse on us, and she didn't want to lose it. I put the cash in my smelly trainer, and we went off to find Mother and Ryan. I looked over and saw them chatting to a man next to a super-classy sports car about fifty feet away. We were about to meet up with them when suddenly I felt something cold and hard touch my head. I turned to see the end of a rifle at eye level. Jane and I were surrounded by armed currency exchangers, also called bandits by Rob. They were shouting at us in their native tongue while shoving rifles into our faces and prodding at our shoulders. I didn't know what we had done, but whatever it was had angered them immensely. At that point, I really did believe in my heart and soul that I was going to be dead soon. Suddenly, Mother charged over and started questioning the men. This next part of my life was in slow motion, and there was no sound. All I could see were the angry men waving their weapons about and my mother flipping out at them, her finger wagging in slow motion in their faces and slow-motion pointing to Jane and me. Maybe she would use one of her actor scenarios on them, possibly "You know, you guys look like the three musketeers." I wanted out of this situation fast. I don't know what was said, but a few minutes later, Mother was holding us by the hands and dragging us to the van. The men lowered their weapons and went on their way, looking back now and again with nasty scowls on their faces and muttering horrible sounds under their breath. I was hoping that they were relatives of the man who stole my pee pot.

Once we were safely in the van, Mother asked us what had happened. We told her that we didn't do anything wrong. Jane explained that she had changed her money with them, and then they went all Wild West on us. My mother asked, "What money?" Jane told her it was the ten pounds she had been given some months ago. Evidently the ten-pound note was an older one that could not be easily exchanged from this location. I guess the man who had exchanged the note later realized that it was going to be a hassle to sell. I took the damp exchanged rupees from my shoe and gave them to Mother. She took them from me and told us to wait in the vehicle.

We watched as she approached the bandits again. She found someone who spoke English and explained to the dangerous men with the big guns what had happened. I imagined that she was telling them how sorry she was for having such silly little girls who knew nothing about money and that she had complete respect for them, and their country, and oh, by the way, do you guys know you look like Charlton Heston, John Wayne, and Clint Eastwood, big American film stars? Whatever tactic she used on them, it worked, and she walked back to the van smiling, and so were they. We had managed once again to escape certain death. With all these real life-threatening situations occurring, I didn't need my imagination to conjure up weird or scary scenarios anymore. Our lives were becoming an absurd horror story and a psychological thriller. After that ordeal, I felt sick to my stomach, like I was going to throw up, but I didn't.

Chapter 9

Pakistan

With haste, we started away from the border. It was not even five minutes before we arrived at the actual entrance to the Khyber Pass. I imagine that the quarter-mile trek from the border to the actual pass was designed for people to change their minds about driving through the Khyber and turn around. We stopped the vehicle and stood in front of a large sign warning people not to stop or sleep in remote or lonely places. It advised that people get to Peshawar before nightfall. The sign was so outlandish that Mother grabbed the camera and took a couple of pictures of it, one with Jane and me standing next to it and one alone. While there, we met a Pakistani local who befriended us. He came over and elaborated on the warning sign, saying it was best to travel through the Khyber after six in the morning and before six in the evening because of the bandit danger. He also pointed out that the tires looked pretty awful on the van and said that they were a potential hazard. It was true; they were getting quite worn, and that had been a concern for a while, but not enough to warrant spending a few hundred pounds on them, especially as we were almost to India and on the boat to Australia. Mother figured they would last until then, and we could replace them once in Perth.

We took another picture, this time with the man. I made sure I had my brain-protecting hat on, as it was sweltering as usual, and then we made our way past the warning sign and onto the Khyber Pass. At first, it appeared like most of the other mountain ranges we had gone through, but as we advanced, it was plain to see that these roads were much narrower and the drops even steeper than the previous mountain passes, which I thought couldn't be possible, but here we were on these tapered cuts in the mountains called roads.

I looked out the window over one of the steeper sides to see skeletal remains of different animals and cars strewn all about in the dry, sandy graveyard. If we plummeted here, we probably were not coming back. As we ventured on, we saw the carcass of a fairly new victim. Vultures were already at the scene, picking off bloody pieces of skin and meat. A camel had been carrying a large load and had apparently fallen over the side. Two people in the distance, probably the owners of the animal, were carrying rolled-up belongings. I felt sad that the camel had just died, but there was nothing anyone could do. A few more miles down the twisting dirt trails, we saw a couple of old vehicle frames that had met their end at one time. They had been picked to the chassis and looked much like a dead cow carcass we had seen before the newly death-claimed camel.

For a thirty-odd-mile trip, it was taking forever. Mother had to drive at a snail's pace so that we would not be the next victims of the perilous pass. To make matters worse, every now and then we caught a glimpse of more dreaded bandits on horseback. We were easy pickings. We were the dying animal, and the bandits were the vultures. Unlike the drive through the Afghanistan Mountains, where the men on horseback had stared for a moment and then disappeared, these bandits made me feel really uncomfortable. Their horses were constantly moving their skinny legs like they were anticipating a race. The stories that Rob had told us didn't help much.

As we drove on, small pebbles and debris fell from the higher elevations onto the road in front of the van, and on top of it. It felt as if the bandits were going to land on the van at any moment, but it was not bandits we had to worry about; it was the falling rocks. The Khyber had its own version of an avalanche, which came down as rockslides and landslides. This definitely was not good. This area had not seen rain for years, so the chance of wet sludge coming down on us was very low; however, the ground was so dry that a rockslide seemed more probable. As Mother drove around the rocks, taking us ever so close to the edge, I thought it was over. The feeling in the pit of my stomach made it hard for me to breathe. If we didn't get covered in rocks, fall over the edge, or get killed by bandits, the lack of air to my brain would kill me.

Mother had just estimated that we were over halfway to the exit of the pass, when we heard a horrible blasting sound. At first we thought we were being fired upon, but we quickly realized that one of the tires had blown out. We came to a stop, perched on the edge of a sheer drop and taking up the whole side of the road. We all jumped out to see what had happened. Sure enough, one of the tires had a five-inch gash in it. We didn't have a spare, either. I couldn't believe it. Other travelers we saw on our trip had spare tires on their roofs, or stuck to the back, sides, or front of their vehicles, and some had spares inside the vehicle just in case, but we had nothing. I asked my mother how come we didn't have one. She told me we used to have one that was strategically placed in the back of the van next to the motor where you couldn't see it, but it was used a couple of days before in the accident in Afghanistan. I asked her, "What accident?"

On that occasion, I had been asleep. Mother was driving through Afghanistan in the night, trying to reach a motel or camp to stop at. It had been usual for us to travel behind large vehicles, and this night she was trailing a truck carrying goods from Europe to the Middle East. The truck driver had seen a large piece of metal in the middle of the road and tried to swerve away from it, causing the vehicle to jackknife and end up half on the road and half on the dirt. As soon as the truck swerved away from the metal chunk, Mother drove over the large obstacle, busting open the front tire. We were brought to a halt not far behind the truck. I couldn't believe I didn't wake up through all that! Anyhow, as the truck driver exited his vehicle, he was quickly apprehended by a group of men who were allegedly waiting to loot the goods. Apparently, it was a well-executed trick commonly played on innocent truck drivers for their bounty of merchandise. The only difference this night was that the truck had us following behind it. Ryan and my mother quickly exited the van and began trying to change the tire, but the bolts were stuck on solid, and their flashlights were running out of battery power. The situation was not good. It didn't take long for the men to come over. They demanded that all passengers get out of the van. Jane exited but left me asleep on the back seat. They asked what kinds of belongings we owned. They wanted to know if we had gold, blue jeans, and shoes, and what brands they were. While my family was being questioned, a few of the other men surrounded the van, trying to see what else was inside. Mother told me she thought that the men were going to attack Jane and her, kill Ryan, and take our van. I don't know if she used one of her actor lines or some sort of tactful negotiation, but shortly after, there was a group discussion among the tribesmen. Finally, two of them changed our tire and told us to be on our way and not to look back. I suddenly recalled the night when that occurred and I had awakened to us leaving the scene of the accident. I had looked back to see the commotion as we were driving away. All this time, I had thought we were not directly involved in that collision. The explanation about why we had no spare tire didn't help the current situation or my sense of security, considering we were in the middle of bandit land. So much for luck!

After five minutes of absorbing the sordid details of the Afghanistan accident, I started feeling quite uneasy. I looked up and down the road. There was no one in sight, not on a horse, on a camel, or in a vehicle. I was not certain if the absence of people was good or bad. We just stood there, waiting for someone to come and help us. What else could we do? I figured that even if I hadn't died back at the border or in a raid gone wrong in Afghanistan, I was going to now, because the bandits were close by somewhere, and the day was going to be over in a few hours.

Nothing could be said or done, so Mother moved some of the gear onto the roof of the van and started to make tea. Why not, I guess. We had nowhere else to go. As we sat there drinking our beverage, we saw a small gray dot on a distant road. About ten minutes later, a car stopped. The men inside had no spare, and their vehicle was too small to pull us anywhere. They apologized for not being able to assist us and drove off. We waited and waited, but to no avail, because it seemed that day nobody wanted to drive on the Khyber Pass. I felt that if we didn't make it out of there by nightfall, we were dead. Mother didn't appear too concerned after the first hour, but by the time the second hour had gone by, she seemed unnerved. She said all we needed was faith, and we would be fine.

I held Camel Merlin in my hand and prayed that he would bring us luck. Within a few minutes, we saw a white dot in the distance at the same location that we had seen the gray dot previously. It was like the bend leading to the road to us. As the vehicle approached, we could see that it was a Volkswagen van like ours. Incredibly, it had a spare tire hanging on the front end. As they drew near, we started waving at them. It was pretty silly in retrospect, because there was only one direction they could be going, and that was by us. When the van reached us, we saw that it was Faith and her buddies. We literally had Faith.

They parked behind us on the extremely narrow road and jumped out to greet us. We had not seen them since Iran, but now here they were. It felt so great. We were saved! Such relief came over us as they approached to help. We were all laughs and giggles. They told us we were lucky because they had purchased the spare only a few days before, specifically for the Afghanistan mountain roads and the

Khyber Pass trip. We knew we were fortunate; there was no doubt about that. After all, nobody in their right mind would want to be stranded out here at night, or anytime, for that matter.

The guys worked relentlessly on removing our wheel, but when they brought over the brand-new tire, their faces turned from excitement to sheer disappointment. We were all aghast. The tire they had was from the newer-model Volkswagen and did not fit. The Dinosaur had a four-lug bolt pattern, and the newer Volkswagen had five. There was no way we were fitting a square peg in a round hole. By this time, the sun was glowing red and soon would be over the mountains to the west. Everyone was speechless. On the one hand, we couldn't let them get caught up in our problem and be out there at night; but on the other, we didn't want to be left there.

Suddenly, Patrick remembered that they had a tire repair kit. It was not really meant for such big tears, but with the alternative being imminent danger, they decided to patch up the tire as best as they could. By the time the sun was beginning to rest on the mountaintops, we were on our way. We thanked Faith and her friends and bid them good-bye. We knew they would have to hurry, and that it would only slow them down if they waited for us. They said they would watch out for us, and if we were not out by one hour after them, they would tell the police. Those were really encouraging words, and once again, I felt impending doom looming over us. But Mother was not about to let us get trapped in pitch dark in bandit land, and she drove as fast and carefully as she could, considering the shape the tire was in. There was no way we were going to let Faith out of sight. Fortunately, it didn't take long to get out of the Khyber Pass. We made it just as dusk was settling in. Faith had been watching us in her rearview mirror and knew we were close. When we drove out, they were there waiting for us. We all applauded the fact that we had made it out of there alive. There was a moment of pure relief and happiness. Then we parted ways. No good-byes this time.

Our goal from this point was to make it to Peshawar, then on to Islamabad, through Jammu, and on to India. That evening, we made it to Peshawar. After much-needed sleep, we woke refreshed and ready for whatever else could go wrong in our lives. The first matter at hand was to buy a new tire for the van. We went about the city looking for one that would fit our vehicle, but there were no tire dealerships anywhere. Eventually, we found a garage that had a few old spare parts lying around. I imagined that most of them were from the pickings in the Khyber. Miraculously, one part they did have was a tire from an older-model Volkswagen. It was not in great shape, and it was somewhat dry-looking, but it was much better than the patched-up tire we were driving on. Luck was on our side, and after a few minutes of compulsory bartering, we had us a tire. As soon as it was fitted on the van, we were off again, this time to Islamabad.

Back when we were at the Pakistan border, Mother had made friends with a man called Ali Khan. He worked as a car driver. All he had to do was drive expensive new cars that people had bought in Europe or nearby countries and deliver them to customers in Pakistan. That was it. He was paid quite a substantial amount for doing this, and considering the risks, I guess it was worth it for the owners of the vehicles. The car Ali was driving was the ritzy deal we had seen at the border. He had taken interest in the fact that Mother had decided to travel across land to Australia. It was not unusual by now for strangers to ask why we were in their respective countries. Ali Khan had been tickled to think that anyone would take such a trip with children. I am pretty certain I could think of another word for how I felt about it, and it was not tickled in the least, especially after the blowout, the border incident, the drug dealers, and the awful rain in Iran. These were not happy times. Anyhow, Ali said that when we made it to Islamabad, we could stay over at his house and visit for a few days to take it easy, relax, and enjoy the country. We could meet his wife and family and catch up on the chatter. He wanted to show us around some tourist sites in Islamabad and let us see all the beauty of his country. After all we had been through, Mother accepted his kind offer. So now we were on our way to Islamabad.

We arrived at Ali Khan's place in the late afternoon. When we reached his house, we found a distraught Mr. Khan. While he was away on business, his wife had left him and taken most of the belongings and furniture. He welcomed us to his home, but we stayed only one night, as we felt uncomfortable with the sad situation. We felt terrible for him. He understood that it was not our responsibility and apologized that he could not take us sightseeing like he had wanted to. We thanked him for his kindness and went on our way.

The next day, we met up with Faith, Patrick, and Keith at a nearby campsite. We would have one last day with them in Islamabad before we truly did go our separate ways. Later that afternoon, Faith and Patrick returned from a shopping trip in town. They had bought massive watermelons in the market. They were fresh and juicy, and that evening, we all sat around and had a watermelon party. Keith was taking the watermelon pieces and putting them to his face like a huge smile. We started thinking of all the things you could do with a watermelon; we were all just goofing around and having a relaxed, memorable moment. Mother took out her camera and used up the last frames for this occasion.

The merriment turned somber that night, as there was talk about the Sothebys. In theory, they should have been in between Faith and us along the way. Faith had seen them drive by her a few miles before the border. That would have placed them at the Khyber Pass after us but before Faith. We had been stuck up on the mountain for more than three hours and had not spotted them before Faith had arrived. We were concerned, and we hoped that they were safe. We expected that they would meet us here at the camp, but they never arrived. We had their contact information and figured that once we arrived in Australia in a few days, we could try to reach them by phone at their lodgings in India. Faith and Patrick said that they would do the same when they reached their destination. The next morning, we set off in separate directions. It was disappointing to wave good-bye to friends yet again, but we knew that no good-bye was permanent.

A few hours later, we were all excited as we neared the Pakistan/India border. We were going to the Indian city of Amritsar. The Pakistani and Indian people apparently did not have a great relationship with each other, because of years of political, religious, and land-right wars. While we were on the Pakistan side of the border, patrols said that we would be lucky if we could get into India. Mother told them that we had all the paperwork that India required for us to enter and that we should have no problem. They laughed and asked if we had a pass for the vehicle. Mother explained that we didn't need one. After all, that was what she had been told in England by the Indian authorities. The patrolmen told us that was what everyone believed. Mother was confident that the vehicle was not a problem. She had checked it out thoroughly in England and knew the rules. India definitely didn't require a pass. We waved good-bye to the Pakistani patrol as we drove off toward the Indian side of the border.

The inspectors there looked over the paperwork, stamped our passports, and told us to pull over to the side. Naturally, we figured they wanted to do a van search. Instead, a different inspector came over and asked for our vehicle pass. Mother just about passed out. She was flabbergasted. She told him that we didn't need one. He said we did. He said we were very welcome to enter India, only the van would have to stay. We stood there silently for about thirty seconds in anticipation of what Mother was going to say. It was becoming a familiar scene. She was staring directly into the dark eyes of the well-built Indian man, who wore a tan uniform and a red turban. Thirty seconds shouldn't feel like an eternity, but when you're waiting for a reaction, it goes by really slowly. In less than thirty seconds, the wheels usually turned at high speed in Mother's brain. I was waiting for an insightful discourse, similar to the ones that had freed us from the previous negative situations, but instead she silently accepted the verdict, broke off eye contact with the hefty man, and steered us back into the van.

I was somewhat surprised that she had said nothing. It was unnatural for her to admit defeat and give up, but here we were, walking back to the van. It was pretty obvious that we were not just going to leave the Dinosaur and all of our belongings at the Indian border. The inspector probably thought that we would just wrap all our junk in sheets, place the huge bundles on our heads, and travel on foot. I had seen people doing that. I wondered how they could bear all that weight on their skinny necks and still walk with their arms at their sides. It was a mystery, and in no way was it an option for us. We turned back toward the Pakistan border and went back with the proverbial tail between our legs.

We parked the van, and the gentlemen we had been speaking to a few minutes earlier strolled over casually. They were kind of laughing, but at the same time they realized it was a crock that we were not permitted to take the van. They told us that the Indians had been turning people away quite frequently, and they would find any reason not to let someone through, especially those with vehicles. Mother spoke with the men for a while, finding different options that we could take to board a ship to our final destination. It was determined that driving south to Karachi would be the best option. From there, we might be able to find safe passage to Australia for ourselves and the vehicle. We stayed at the border for a few hours while Mother engaged in pleasant conversation with the border patrol. They were really friendly, and they appeared to be concerned for our well-being. They scribbled down a route on our map for us to take to Karachi and advised us to stay at police posts at night for safety. Although we had not thought that safety was an issue in towns and cities, we took the men's advice.

We followed the squiggly line on the map until we arrived at the first suggested stop, Lahore. It was a bustling place with a river that ran through the length of the city. The river itself was an unusually busy area. Women were washing their clothes in the dirty brown water, and others were taking baths. There were children swimming next to oxen that were taken there to get a drink and cool down. It was a community watering hole. I asked if we could go swimming too. Mother was adamantly against such an act. All this traveling, and I had not yet been swimming anywhere. It didn't seem fair, seeing as these countries were hot!

We stopped for only a short time in Lahore. We managed to find a store that sold ice-cold Coke. For a treat, Jane and I were bought a couple of bottles each. We popped off the caps and started gulping down the wonderful carbonated drink as quickly as we could. The fizz burned and came out my nose, but it was so good, I didn't care. Lately it was a rare occasion to find ice-cold anything. We had something to eat, bought some provisions, and went on our way.

At this stage, there were no time restraints for when we arrived in Karachi. All of the original plans had been busted completely. We took several days to get to Karachi, sleeping at police posts at every convenience. At first, we were wary of asking the police to let us stay, but every post welcomed us and gave us outdoor beds called *charbangs* to sleep on. Everyone slept outside, because it was so hot, even at night. Evenings at the police posts were always relaxing. We felt safe. Every night, and at all the posts, you could smell the exotic smell of incense. When I asked what they burned that smelled so good, Ryan told me it was hashish. I was under the belief that hashish was illegal, but clearly that was not an issue here. I speculated that the smell relaxed everyone enough that they could not cause trouble. It was rather unique. I liked it, but Mother always placed me as far away from the heady scent as she could. The only smoke I was allowed to be with was that from the green mosquito repellents we had to light constantly throughout the night, and that stunk. The day after we stayed at the Sadiqabad police post, my mother woke up to find that the repellents had not worked on her and she was covered in mosquito bites. She was the only one who had been attacked so badly, and she was really uncomfortable. We had been given malaria shots and booster pills back in England, but they ran out. Concerned for her health, we took a detour from the squiggly line on our map and stopped in the city of Sukkar.

While in Sukkar, we stayed at the Interpakistan Hotel, where we called for a doctor for Mother. He gave her some pills and told her to rest for a few days. He asked her how she was bitten so badly. She was so embarrassed to say that we slept outside that she told him she didn't know how it had happened. The doctor's visit cost two hundred and twenty-five rupees. Mother was upset about that, but health came before money, and besides, we needed to take a break. It was nice taking a pause from sleeping outdoors. We took real showers and had all our clothes properly washed. It was a time to rest, regroup, and reassess our position. The stay was uneventful but refreshing, and two days later we were on our way to Karachi.

The days had been hotter than usual, and our drinks disappeared fast, even though we tried to conserve the liquids as much as we could. We had an unplanned journey from here on out, and making sure the money was going to last was something of a concern. Drinks of any kind in bottles were a majority of the expense. So we had to make do with what we could, while at the same time avoiding any water from wells.

About one hundred and fifty miles away from Sukkur, we stopped at a small village. We all had to take a potty break. We pulled over to where some villagers were standing and asked them where the toilet was. They pointed out to an area in the field, but we didn't see any old huts or anything that resembled a restroom. We tried to explain what we needed, without being crude. The couple nodded and pointed once again to the field. On closer inspection, we saw that a few others were completing their potty breaks. I thought that a reptile-ridden, feces-smeared, stinky hut with no toilet paper or water was bad, but this was worse, by far. My mother concurred. Unfortunately, when you have to go, you have to go, so Jane, Ryan, and I had no problems doing what we had to. Mother was embarrassed and needed Ryan to hold a towel around her so no one could see. This act caused the whole village to be interested. She would have been better off just doing her stuff in the open.

After we exited the field, it appeared that the whole community had come out to see the alien family. They graciously welcomed us with smiling faces, offering us food and water. Some went over to the communal pump and started to draw out cold water while others brought over cups to drink from. One man who spoke a very small amount of English told us that the water was good and fresh. We all gulped down the divine water and splashed it over our faces and in our hair to cool us from the insane heat. With that, the villagers crowded around and started pulling us in the direction of a communal bath. It was a five-foot by seven-foot cement hole in the ground that had a huge faucet with well water running in it. Everyone scurried out and away from the pool of water so that we could use it. Understanding that Mother was shy, they all left us to bathe in comfort. It was wonderful, the closest thing to a swimming pool that we had encountered. It had green algae growing around the walls, and it wasn't chlorinated or fancy, but it felt so good. After we dried off and were back in fresh clothing, we had to be on our way to get to the next police post before nightfall. Mother offered the villagers money for their kindness, but they refused. They just bid us good-bye, and we drove away.

That night, we slept at a police post near Hyderabad. When we woke up the next morning, none of us felt that well. We started off toward Karachi, but we all needed to go to the toilet almost constantly. Every fifteen minutes or so, we were using the communal potty fields to do our thing, or at least we hoped they were potty fields. There was nothing stopping us from what we had to do. By the time we reached Karachi, we were dehydrated and throwing up, and we had fevers. It was so bad. We were driving around the new city, desperate to find somewhere to stay. We found a hostel for travelers, but it was full. A young hippie couple staying there heard we were looking for a place to lodge. They advised us to go to the Karachi YMCA and find shelter there. Evidently, there were family units available as long as a male was in the family. We started toward the facility immediately, hoping we could get a place to lie down and recover from whatever it was we had picked up.

Part II

Twists and Turns

Chapter 10

Karachi

We dashed out of the van and into the lobby of the YMCA. There was a disturbance outside with a particularly threatening dog. Evidently, it was a female protecting its puppies. A couple of men were trying to move her away from the front of the building. I supposed a crazed dog didn't look good for business, although I felt kind of sad for the animal, as probably she was just looking for food for her babies. I was glad we made it inside without incident, though.

When we entered the foyer, there was another tumult that involved a rather oversized rat and a maintenance man. The poor chap was chasing the massive rodent around, trying to catch it to put it outside. From the looks of things, the rat was winning. Moments later, the receptionist came out and apologized for the stir. We were not upset by the scene, as we had already seen so much worse. All we wanted to do was get a room.

Mother had rushed in and headed straight for the toilet. After the bathroom break, she came back all upset because she had seen a lizard on the wall. She had hit the poor thing in a panic and broken off its tail. I knew exactly how it felt having a reptile in the bathroom and was actually glad she had been through that experience, just so she could see how upsetting it really was. The receptionist told Mother that she didn't have to feel bad, as the tails of that particular lizard dropped off as a natural defense, and it would soon grow a new one. I thought that to be rather clever, but then I realized that the specimen Mother had encountered was about ten times smaller than the beast that had jumped out at me back in Afghanistan, which for sure had not been a tail-dropping newt! I was momentarily disappointed that she had run into such a small animal, but I was quickly distracted by the affirmation of room rental. This place was more like a zoo than lodgings, but as long as it had nice rooms with beds and a proper, seated throne, I didn't care.

Soon we booked in, and that night a doctor was called. We were told that our fevers, vomiting, severe dehydration, and diarrhea were possibly due to cholera, amoebic dysentery, or any number of bacterial or parasitic infections that one could contract from drinking well water. The actual cause was never diagnosed, but we were prescribed a number of medications to take over the next few weeks. I couldn't understand how the villagers didn't get sick from bathing in and drinking the well water, but we were. I also couldn't understand why they called it "well water" when in fact it made one anything but well.

Regardless of the how or why, we stayed sick for days. Ryan suffered the most. He was in so much discomfort that he couldn't get out of bed. I would go in and check on him, but all he could do was lie there. I felt quite bad for him, as several days had gone by, and we girls had recovered, but he still was sick with the runs. Later, my mother found out that he had been taking a medication for constipation along with the prescribed pills. He thought it would help his stomach, but in fact the medication made him worse. She kind of teased him about that, but he found it no laughing matter. While he was resting and trying to pull through, my mother, Jane, and I would go out to the lobby and meet new people.

One afternoon, we were leaving our quarters to meet a professor we had met a few days earlier. He was going to give us a tour of the University of Karachi, where he was a full-time faculty member. As we walked through the long corridor that led to the huge lobby where he was supposed to meet us, we heard a commotion. On further inspection, we noticed a film crew setting up their equipment. Being curious, Mother asked one of the members what they were doing. A production manager came over and introduced himself as Servia. Delighted that we were curious about his work, he began to convey the details of the project.

He was filming a commercial, and he had one of Pakistan's top advertisement models and actresses there to promote the new summer prints for a company called Bonanza Fabrics. The young model was very attractive and had long black hair. We watched in awe as they repeatedly filmed the girl lip-synching to a jingle. They played it over and over, but she was having problems, as she didn't speak English, and the song was, unfortunately, in English.

It was quite intriguing watching filmmaking, and while the crew continued their work, Servia became interested in us. Mother introduced me and Jane to him. At first he was confused because he thought Jane was a boy. It had been an ongoing joke for me, because I thought it was funny that everyone thought she was a boy. She was very tall for her age, even taller than Mother, and she had short hair. She was pretty, but if you glanced at her instead of taking a good look, she appeared boyish. Jane was actually fine with that and admitted that she was a tomboy. She had bragged about that even at school in England.

After a short chat, Servia looked back at the crew, shook his head, and respectfully withdrew from the conversation, to assist with the frustrating commercial situation. Eventually, the professor arrived and took a seat in the waiting area. We approached him, and shortly after, we began leaving the lobby. Jane loved music, and she could remember all the words to a new song the day it came out. She knew all the lyrics to every song we had ever listened to in England, and all the words to the songs of her favorite band Sparks, and their music was bizarre to me. It bothered me that I couldn't remember any words from songs. I could always hum the tune, but I remembered no lyrics. While traveling, we rarely heard English songs, so when Jane heard the commercial tune, she had it promptly embedded in her brain. Jovially she sang the ditty as we exited the building.

We settled into the Dinosaur and started on our way to tour the university campus. The professor was extremely proud of the facility, and he mentioned how it was one of the few truly prestigious educational institutions in Pakistan. On our way, he described some of the sites we would see, including newly constructed buildings, park areas, and the recent addition of a botanical garden on the university grounds. It sounded like it was really interesting, and I was looking forward to the outing.

I noticed that Mother was a tad distracted, intermittently taking her eyes away from the road ahead to look in her rearview mirror. She had a frown on her forehead that told me that the jeep men from Iran had miraculously found us. I didn't want to look back. She didn't alert anyone to her suspicions, but I knew something was up. Every now and then, she politely smiled and nodded at the professor as he rambled on about the history of Pakistan. At the same time, we were picking up speed. We took a few detours, and finally the frown disappeared.

Just when I thought everything was fine, we came to a roadblock formed by a row of police cars. We came to a screeching halt in the middle of the road. Several policemen exited their cars and approached us. It was excruciatingly hot, and you could see their reflections on the road as the rising heat distorted their images from the ground up. It was a slow-motion moment, similar to the one I had experienced before at the border. The familiar sick feeling came to my stomach as a million scenarios entered my head. I looked over at the professor, who was clutching his seat. He looked shocked and glanced back at Mother with an "I am not with her" look on his face. The world went silent momentarily as the police moved toward the vehicle. We all sat there motionless, not knowing what to expect. It seemed like an eternity went by before one of the immaculately uniformed police officers was at the window.

Before he could say anything, a large white van pulled up behind the police vehicles. Servia, the man we had met just moments before in the YMCA, jumped out and ran toward us. The initial horrified expression on Mother's face turned to a puzzled look as Servia approached the window, which was open as usual on account of the heat. The policeman nodded and then instructed the fleet of police to leave. Servia was out of breath from the sprint in the searing heat. He said he had been trying to chase us down since we left the YMCA because he wanted to ask Mother if Jane could do the commercial for him. We all sighed in relief, especially the professor. I was still nauseated from thinking that we were being chased down by bad guys, but I was glad that it was something good for a change. After a few minutes of deliberation between Jane and Mother, an agreement was made with our new friend Servia to make a commercial in the following days.

Early the next morning, Servia came to the YMCA to meet with Mother and Jane to discuss what she would do in the commercial. The primary reason Servia wanted Jane to do the advert was because she could sing in English. He knew that she wouldn't have difficulty lip-synching to the melody of "Moving Colors," the song created for the commercial. Jane was lovely, and Servia knew that she would look stunning on screen. But there was the problem of her short hair. Most women in Pakistan had long hair; it was a mark of attractiveness. In order to combat this issue, scarves were made from the fabrics that she could drape around her hair and neck, hiding the fact that she did not possess the locks of Rapunzel. The shooting of part of the commercial placed Jane on top of the van. Not only was Jane going to be in a commercial, but so was the Dinosaur! We told Ryan about the commercial people, but he was not interested.

After Ryan recovered, he became extremely aloof. Mother had been the leader on this mission, but as second-in-command, Ryan had not contributed anything to improve our situation. His answer to all problems was to go back to England. He was convinced that returning was the only solution to our dilemma. The relationship between Mother and Ryan became strained, and before long, we were not having any communication with him. It was perplexing. When we would pass him in the cafeteria, we had to behave as though we didn't know each other. If eye contact was made, a nod of acknowledgement was all that was called for, just as one might react to a newcomer at the YMCA. Soon we hardly saw him at all, but Mother was determined to complete the mission, and nothing was going to stop her, especially not Ryan.

Over the weeks, a curious change came over Mother, and before long, she had a following. Mother had no shortage of acquaintances. Everyone treated her like she was royalty. She even had a male servant called Kanji, who bowed down and did anything for her. In fact, it was the same gentleman we had seen chasing the huge rat the night we checked in. He was a sweet man who probably looked older than his actual age. He was very thin and walked with a very slight hunchback appearance, as he was constantly in servitude mode. He was married to a younger wife and had ten children, with the recent news of another one on the way. My mother was kind to him. She often offered him rupees for helping her with translation, shopping, and as a general guide to Karachi, but he always refused the money until she insisted it was for the new baby. He would nod sideways and place his hands together as if in prayer. That was how he said thank you.

It was extremely convenient knowing him, as he lived really close to the grounds of the YMCA. He was our go-to guy. When we needed anything, we went to Kanji. He became more than a servant to us, though. We all considered him a good friend, and we went to his home and visited with his huge family frequently. They lived in a U-shaped court area that was divided up into different rooms by hanging grass mats. All the children slept on the floor on woven rugs in these cubicles, while the adults had the wood-and-rattan cots called *charbangs* to sleep on. Even though everyone back in England would have thought that these were awful conditions, the family was content. Kanji and his wife lived and worked at the YMCA. That was their life, and like the people in the villages, they didn't know any other way and accepted their life as it was.

While at the YMCA, which we now called the Y, we met so many wonderful people and different characters. It was normal for me to wander about the place and chat with everyone. As long as I did not leave the grounds or venture into the male lodging area, I could go where I wanted. The Y had a big open space outside in the court area where hens ran around. If you wanted a chicken curry, you just pointed to the bird you wanted, and forty minutes or so later, you were eating it. The court was also home to the wild dog that had very young puppies. The cafeteria staff occasionally threw out scraps for her to eat. On the other end of the court, and up in an area that had what looked like a huge bird's nest, was a cat that had given birth to some kittens. I was allowed to view them but was told absolutely not to touch them for any reason. Rabies was a big problem here too, so befriending the animals was forbidden. I really wished I could have them as pets and constantly nagged my mother for them. No matter what I said, the answer was no—quite right, too, considering the risks.

One day I went out there and saw one of the puppies squirming away from the others. The mother was nowhere to be seen, so I went over and picked up the chubby little puppy whose eyes were still closed. He was so adorable, and I wanted him so badly, but I put him back with the others. Suddenly, Kanji grabbed me and was scolding me in broken English and Urdu. He took me to my mother, and I was forbidden to go out in the court while the dogs and cats were there. Later, the animals were taken away because they kept trying to eat the chickens. I was told that if I wanted to play out there, I could now, but I saw no point.

We had been at the Y for a while, and I wasn't sure when we were going to get a boat to Australia. I felt hopelessly bound to the place and wondered if we would ever get to Perth or if I would see my Nan again. I wanted to ask Mother, but I knew I was better off just waiting to see what happened, because she was in control of the situation. I felt we were just roaming about with no real goal. It was frustrating, and I felt very insecure. I was also bored out of my mind most of the time.

Since the animals were gone, it had been a while since I had played outside. One afternoon, I was fed up, so I ventured out to the courtyard. Covering the grounds were hundreds of dead dragonflies. I bent down and picked up one of the huge, dry insects to have a better look at it. This was another new experience for me, because never in my life had I seen such a big dragonfly. While I was taking in all the details of the crispy critter, a cook came over from the cafeteria and picked one up. He threw it up in the air and let it fall to the ground. The poor dead creature spun as it fell to its resting place. The cook didn't speak very much English but was smiling and saying it was a helicopter. He was trying to tell me that if you found one alive you could tie a piece of string to it and make it look like a kite. He threw a few more up into the air and then left abruptly, as he was called back to the kitchen.

I remembered a time when I was back in England. I threw sycamore seeds into the air, much the same way, and watched them rotate as they fell; but this seemed cruel, as they were living at one time, and tying a piece of string to a living thing seemed more like torture than fun. I took the dragonfly I was holding and placed it on a nearby bush overlooking its dead relatives. I sat there for a while, deep in thought, and then Jane came over from the cafeteria and asked me what I was doing. Briefly I explained the situation.

She said I looked sad but told me she had found something that would make me happy. I had to guess which hand she had the mysterious happy thing in. Every time I picked a hand, I was wrong, until finally she gave in and passed me the ball that I had misplaced weeks ago in France. We threw it around a few times and then returned inside. I was glad I had one of my favorite toys back, but I suspected that Jane had known all along where the ball had been.

Since meeting Servia, Mother had met several influential folk, especially those in advertising. Servia's advertisement was different, because the Pakistani film industry was on the horizon of making the first moving color commercials to be shown in between the films at the cinema, as opposed to the regular black-and-white ads or stills. The very first moving commercial in color was the fabric advertisement that Jane had now completed. The industry had taken an interest in Jane after the production viewing and asked if she could be the model for several other commercials. At first, Mother was skeptical. We still had no evidence that it was the real deal. Jane had been paid a small amount for the job, but we still had not seen the commercial for ourselves. Servia was pushing for an answer for her to work on a project for a paint company. Mother agreed, and the next shooting date was set. I was allowed to go with them while they were shooting. It was all glamour and fame for Jane, quite extraordinary. Sometimes I had to stay with Kanji and his family, and that was fine with me, because being around all those adults was quite often boring for me.

After a few days of shooting some stills for Jane's portfolio, we were invited to the premiere showing of the first commercial she had done, which was for the fabric company. We sat in the cinema, looking up at the big screen, waiting to watch *The Magnificent Men and Their Flying Machines,* when suddenly there was Jane, my sister, up on the big screen, being a model. It suddenly struck me that this was reality. I thought it was really funny and surreal. I was smiling so hard, my face hurt. I felt really proud. It was so cool seeing my sister up there. Obviously, Mother was proud as well. She almost had tears in her eyes. When I looked over at Jane, she looked more surprised than anything else. She suddenly felt exposed and wanted to leave, just in case someone recognized her. I wanted to see it again, and I asked Servia if they would replay it. He just smiled at me and went on to talk to another adult. I never saw that commercial on the big screen again, but seeing it in the theater that evening was proof that Jane was a real model.

Chapter 11

Rich Man, Poor Man

Mother and Jane frequently were out managing Jane's new career and shooting more commercials. These days were long, so I stayed at the Y, or with Kanji's family. I was never in any danger, as everyone treated us all with the utmost respect. I started wandering into the games area, where the old Pakistani men who worked at the Y taught me how to play chess. There was one man called Iqbar. He was an ex-cricket player for the Pakistan team, but was also an excellent chess player. He helped me to master the art of chess. Before long, I was beating the old men at their own game. There was a billiard table too, but I was not allowed to play with that. Iqbar had taught Jane how to play, but I was too small. Chess was a lot of fun, but when evening came, I had to return to the family lobby.

On those evenings, we spent time surrounded by different people. Since many of the males now knew Jane was a girl and a screened model, she had accumulated devotees of her own. The Y lobby was a community meeting place, and most evenings, it was full of people and lots of fun. There was one young Pakistani man who worked cleaning the rooms in the daytime. At night, he'd come out dressed in a pink *salwar kameez* and dance around with his lacy sarong. He was quite funny. It didn't matter if there were girls or guys around. He just sang and danced in front of people, and rubbed his back up against theirs. He cracked me up. I thought he was hilarious. I was told that he was a eunuch. I learned that was a person who was born a boy but was no longer one. He acted like a girl and was called Betty, so I saw him as a girl. *Baiti* is also the Urdu word for "daughter," so his name was appropriate. One night, I mimicked him, dancing around like he did, and found myself in a whole bunch of trouble. A male guest had playfully thrown me a rupee, and that had my mother up in rut. It was not long before I was not allowed to be out there at night. On those occasions, I stayed in our room with a young woman called Beena. She kept me company until my mother and Jane returned.

Mother had met Beena at the Y. Beena was in love with one of the men who worked there. She wanted to marry him but was engaged by arrangement to another man. That really upset her, but she was always upset or worried about something, and she often visited so she could talk with Mother and be consoled by her words. One day, she came in talking about how hot it had been and how Pakistan had been in a four-year drought that was causing major problems with the crops, the water supply, and the economy. She said she wanted to pray for rain, but on the other hand, too much rain brought many problems because of the poor drainage in Karachi. What were they going to do? Mother told her not to worry, as rain followed her everywhere she went, and if Beena wanted rain, it would eventually come. Thinking back on all the rain we had seen, especially in Iran, I was inclined to agree. Still, I thought making such a rainy claim was a bit much. I could not imagine what the consequences would be if they had a five-year drought. Apart from constantly worrying about this and that, Beena was a really nice person, one of many awesome people we met at the Y.

One sunny afternoon I was outside in the Y parking lot with a male guest who was camping in his van. He didn't have a room but was allowed to park on the property, quite close to where we had the Dinosaur parked. He was a pleasant man from Holland. Naturally, I loved his accent. In fact, I loved all the different accents, but his was similar to those from the traveling hotel we had seen in Iran. His name was Aldarik, but he said I could call him Al. He had a mop of dirty blond hair and blue eyes, and he wore a shell necklace around his neck. He wore cut-off jeans and leather sandals. He reminded me of the hippie couple back at the hostel.

When I strolled up, he was sitting in the rear of his van with the hatchback door flipped up and his legs dangling over the edge of the bumper. He was rolling a cigarette in a strange contraption, with green tobacco. I told him it was the prettiest color of tobacco I had ever seen. He told me it wasn't tobacco but a plant called cannabis. It meant nothing to me. While I was there talking with him, he looked at my scalp and told me I had spiders in my hair. I wondered what in the world he was talking about. He lit up his green cigarette and started telling me about his home and his travels, and then from nowhere my mother appeared in hysterics. She asked Aldarik what he was doing. He told her that he was smoking weed and telling me about Holland. She pulled me away and told me to say good-bye to Al. Disappointed,

I turned and waved good-bye. As we were walking away, he shouted out to Mother that I had spiders in my hair.

When we returned to the room, she asked what he meant by that. I shrugged my shoulders, as I didn't know what he was rambling on about. She checked in my hair to find that I had masses of lice crawling about. She grabbed my hand, and we were off to Kanji's for help. When we arrived, Kanji's wife, Lata, was already sitting cross-legged on a mat, combing out lice from one of her children's heads. I assumed I had picked them up there. Mother showed Kanji my head, and within minutes, I was the one sitting on the floor, having my hair picked at. I felt like a chimpanzee.

As of late, we had not seen Ryan very much. Mother had not spoken to him for weeks. It didn't help matters that Ryan did nothing to pursue the situation. Knowing how the trip had come to a halt, I thought he would at least try to intervene and come up with a brilliant idea to complete our goal of making it to Australia. After all, that was why we were there. Even though there had been no communication with him for weeks, seeing Ryan in the cafeteria or in the lobby once in a while made me feel secure, like eventually it would all get better. But one day I found out that Ryan had left. The fact that he had abandoned us all alone in Pakistan did not appear to faze Mother one iota. I, on the other hand, was devastated. It was not like we were extremely close or that I even talked to him very much when we were a family, but he was familiar. The idea that he could help himself and not us, hurt. I felt abandoned. Mother received word from England that Ryan was going to petition for a divorce.

Life went on after Ryan left, and all three of us girls had made many close friends in the time we had been at the Y. We were constantly meeting new people because of the nature of the lodgings. Mother met a local gentleman called Malik. He was very charming, and once in a while he took us out to eat to expensive restaurants. I was having a really hard time adjusting to the food, and I could eat only certain items. He used to bring me cold bottles of mango juice that I drank down in a few seconds, despite its thick consistency, because it was so good and it was something my stomach could tolerate. Once in a while, he took us to a really awesome Chinese restaurant a couple of miles away from the Y, where I could eat most of the food with no problems. The restaurant itself was really stylish, with a deep red carpet. There were black tables and chairs covered with crispy white tablecloths, and lovely Chinese lanterns hung from the ceiling over each one. It had excellent air conditioning, which was so good that I was told to take a cardigan with me when we went there. The smell of the food cooking was so blissful that I wished I lived there.

The first time we went to eat there was insane. There were six in our party, and while we were deciding what we would have as our main course, I decided to have my favorite, won ton soup, as a starter. Everyone thought that was a good idea and agreed to have the same appetizer. About ten minutes later, six huge family-size tureens came out. It was enough soup to feed about forty people! We asked the waiters why they had brought out so much, and they said that was what we had ordered. Apart from the huge misunderstanding, the food was wonderful; however, it was rather pricey, so we ate there on rare occasions.

Malik also helped Mother organize parties on the beach at a shoreline called Hox Bay. That was another great time for me to have food that was agreeable. We rented a beach house that had a kitchen with a wood-burning stove. Everyone brought something to cook. Malik made delicious curries that were milder so I could actually eat them. One of these beach parties was especially memorable. I am not sure what made it so special, but I remember it well. A whole bunch of friends and acquaintances from the Y met up at the beach house in the early afternoon. Everyone was getting their cooking time in and making all kinds of scrumptious food.

I enjoyed being by the ocean. I played a crazy game with myself, in which I walked on the scorching-hot sand until I couldn't take it anymore and then ran as fast as I could to cool off my burning feet in the cool ocean water.

I should have been scared of the Pakistan waters, as earlier that month, Jane and I had been splashing around by the ocean edge when something stung both of us around our ankles. We screamed and ran for our lives, but we could not see what had stung us. Mother said it might have been an electric eel or a jellyfish. We should have known that the unfamiliar waters could be dangerous, because before the stinging day, we had a dangerous run-in with huge water turtles. Mother had said she thought she saw something like huge wooden treasure chests bobbing about in the water, but none of us could see anything. We all went out to take a swim in the very rough waters to find out we were bouncing back and forth between sea turtles. The turtles themselves did not attack us, but the nature of the huge waves had us bumping into them. On this day of the party, though, I had no intentions of entering the water, no matter what. It was beginning to get dark, and I didn't want find out what the night ocean held.

As dusk was descending upon us, everyone began settling down for the night. People crashed on the beach, in the beach house, and on the roof. I was looking for a place to settle, and I decided to go on the roof with some of the other people. Just when I was about to rest, my mother came and told me it was better for me to sleep in the van or downstairs with her, instead of upstairs, where there were mostly men. I decided to take the keys and crash out in the van.

When I stepped out of the beach house, I noticed that the moon was shining brightly in the perfectly dark blue sky. The moonlight shimmered on the surface of the shadowy sea, which randomly cast up seemingly white waves. Now and then, I could see the massive heads of the sea turtles bobbing in and out of the water. I was told it was egg-laying season, and soon the females would come up to shore and leave hundreds of eggs under the sand. I decided to take a walk to see if I could spot any of them.

It was a bit creepy, as the night shore was very different from the daytime. In the day, the shore appeared empty and sandy except for the occasional seagull that made a screeching noise to announce its arrival, but at night, the beach was covered with small crabs. As I walked along the shoreline, the crabs scurried into little holes in the sand. When I passed them, they came back out again. While walking along the beach, I was surrounded by the strange animals. They were making a perfectly circular path for me to walk in that was about six feet in diameter, no matter what the direction was. I felt like the little mermaid taking her first steps on the beach. I had to step carefully so I didn't crunch any of the tiny stragglers that were graciously making a path for me.

Finally, I found a spot to sit down. I sat on the damp sand and looked out at the ocean. I could still hear some of the party group laughing in the distance. A slight smell of food wafted in the air, mixed with jasmine and gardenia flowers. I looked back toward the beach house to see a few guests still sitting by a dwindling log fire that had been blazing so much earlier that evening that no one could stand by it, but now it was peaceful and serene. That night I felt at one with nature, until the curious critters began to get too friendly and started crawling over my feet. I looked around to find that I was completely surrounded by crabs. My circular path had disappeared. I was completely freaked out at the sight and screeched my way up the beach until I made it to the van. Once safely in the Dinosaur, I laughed at myself for running away from the harmless crabs. My heart was thumping hard inside my chest, and I was out of breath, but I felt content.

The next morning when I woke up, everyone was already awake. Eggs were being served up from the van's faithful propane stovetop, and cups of tea and coffee were being handed around. It had been a really neat party that began the day before and was still going on the next morning. How cool was that?

I stretched my legs and looked down the beach. There was no sign of the busy crabs anywhere, as more than likely they hid in the safety of their holes, away from hungry seagulls, during the day. There were, however, men racing along the beach on camels. I was so astounded at the sight of the magnificent animals bounding along at high speeds. I had only seen camels walking really slowly and thought of them as a toting kind of animal, as opposed to a race animal. I asked my mother if I could go down and ride on one. At first she was unsure and a little reluctant to find out, but after breakfast was over, my mother and Malik took me down to pet the camels.

A few minutes later, I was being lifted onto one of the massive animals, which had kneeled down so I could sit on a special camel saddle. It was all fun and games until he stood up. I was scared, being up so high above the ground, and when the animal started galloping along the beach, I was more than scared; I was petrified. I hung as tight as I could onto the leather straps tied on the camel's head, and although I was afraid, I began to enjoy the ride. The adrenalin rush must have taken away my fear, and before long, I wanted to keep galloping along the beach as far as the camel would take me. This was one of those thrilling moments my mother had told me I would have. I had been allowed to ride the camel as a courtesy, but the camel races were real. I wanted to own one and become a camel jockey, but that was not going to happen.

In addition to taking us to eat and organizing social meetings, Malik also took us around the business area where he worked. He showed us his office building and other places that he frequented, including showy stores and modern-tech Art Nouveau high rises. In some parts of the buildings and streets, the walls were covered in nasty reddish-brown stains that made it like someone had been shot up against them. It was really gross and somewhat scary. I asked Malik why there was blood on the walls, and he told me that it wasn't blood; it was a stain from a kind of herbal chew called *paan*. Apparently, *paan* chewing was used in daily rituals or for mouth cleansing. I wasn't exactly sure what it was all about, even after it was explained to me. All I knew was that they needed to spit that crud somewhere else and not on all the walls. It was like walking through a house of horrors.

In truth, though, the *paan* chewing was the least of horrors, when it came down to it. One day was extremely memorable for me. It wasn't because of the *paan* stains, the tall modern buildings, or the many shopping areas with their colorful inventory of items; it was the absolutely horrible conditions in which the impoverished children had to endure that left a lasting impression. As we walked around the streets, we saw beggars and homeless people in all the crevices and spaces available living between buildings. Women came out and pinched their babies' arms to make them cry or, even worse, purposely injured them seriously to get sympathy from bystanders. There were adults who were blind, had no legs, or had only one arm. Malik told us that their owners had probably done that to them when they were small children. It was so horrible that I wanted to cry.

I saw one toddler, maybe two years old, who had full casts on both of her legs. She had to sit in a permanent splits position. Her mother was sitting on the side of the road, rocking back and forth, with the child sitting next to her. She held out her hand for money while chanting and groaning in the most awful manner, and the baby was crying. I told Malik to give them money, but he refused and told us that the begging was a business. He that said one week out of every year the beggars were permitted to go into banks and exchange all their bags of small change for large bills. He told us that most of those people had more cash after the trade-in than a man working full-time at a regular job for a year. Although it was excruciatingly painful to see children living like that, we were not allowed to contribute to this world of corruption and exploitation. I had seen the beggars from the van many times, but it was a very different scene on foot. Malik took us away from all that and apologized for putting me through it. For him, this was normal, and it had not occurred to him that it would be such a difficult thing for my mother and me to witness. He wanted to make it up to us and decided that he would arrange a more joyful occasion.

Later that day, we went to the Karachi zoological gardens. It was a definite improvement from the busy city. There were lush, green gardens, and it was peaceful. Most of the animals sat lazily in their habitats, chewing on scraps of food or just happily napping. A female Indian elephant threw straw and dirt on her back. Now and again, she picked up a huge stack of straw and threw it at visitors. Apparently, the elephant brought many visitors to the zoo because she was so entertaining.

After we had spent about an hour there, it began to get too hot, so we decided to leave. It seemed to me that these animals were treated better than the beggars I had seen recently. I couldn't understand how there could be such huge gaps within the social and economic structure of the people. Politics was another one of those subjects about which I was not enlightened, and quickly I decided that maybe I should not question the running of a country. After all, I knew I probably couldn't do it. It just bothered me knowing that some of the other countries we had visited didn't have such poverty, and I wondered why it was so bad here. One thing I did know was that, while we might be in a sticky situation, at least I was not one of those poor children sleeping in the streets.

Malik was always willing to show us some new aspect of Pakistani culture. It was a welcome eye-opener for me. I loved going on day trips to see what was happening outside the Y. One evening, Malik took us to see an Indian movie called *Raja Jani*. Before the movie began, the Pakistan national anthem played. Everyone stood up except for Mother and me. She said that it was not Her Royal Majesty the Queen's anthem, so she didn't see the point. Malik instructed us to stand up and pay respect to Prime Minister Zulfikar Ali Bhutto, or someone else would, and it would come in the form of a violent kick in the back. I shot up into standing position and looked behind me to see some upset ushers coming toward us. In an effort to prevent an altercation, Mother reluctantly stood up. The ushers backed off, and we stood as still as possible until it was time to sit. That was the first encounter I experienced that gave me an indication of what the person who ran the country was like. I took a few seconds to think about this Mr. Bhutto, and then I went on to watch the movie.

The film lasted about three hours and did not have subtitles. Malik was constantly leaning over to tell us what was happening. The story was about a long-lost princess who was thought to be dead as a child. Years later, the queen mother was told that the princess was alive, but it was a lie told by villains to get to the royal treasure. It turned out that the girl was the real princess after all, so it was a happy ending for the queen mother and the newly returned princess. The movie had a lot of dancing and singing, which is the nature of Indian and Pakistani movies. I liked the sound of the songs but never understood what they meant. Malik sang the songs to my mother and tried to teach me to sing them. I learned some of the lyrics, but I still didn't know what I was singing about. Anyhow, after the movie was over, I wished that I was secretly a princess and that I would be whisked off to a beautiful palace with tables of food and riches beyond belief. That idea went away pretty quickly, though, as I knew I was nothing but an English kid in Pakistan.

A few weeks later, we had another beach party. Organizing one of these parties was not just a matter of going to one grocery store for all your needs and driving down to the seaside. It took quite a bit of planning. First of all, Malik had to make sure the beach house was available. Once that was confirmed, we would go to the outdoor marketplace and pick up all the food fresh. The market smelled repulsive, but if we wanted food, that was where it was. The vendors threw any rotten fruit or vegetables on the street. Wild dogs and cats would come out to eat the fly-infested food. Apart from the dogs and cats, all manner of animals roamed around: chickens, goats, cows, donkeys, and camels. It was not unusual to see them doing their thing in the middle of the filthy streets. We had to be very careful where we stepped much of the time.

Meat was bought on the butcher side of the market, where it was cut up right there and sold. It sat out in the heat, where flies took their lunch breaks. The flies also laid their eggs on the cuts of meat, so we had to make sure that we cleaned it thoroughly before cooking. The meat variety consisted of mutton, beef, lamb, chicken, and goat. We were told that if we were lucky, we might get a choice of horse meat. I didn't feel that was very lucky, especially for the poor horse. Anyway, we mostly opted for chicken, but this time Malik also wanted to make a beef curry, so we bought both. It was chopped up right there on the huge, bloodstained chopping board and wrapped in neat paper packages. If really fresh chicken was on the menu, we would have needed to take a cage with us, but thankfully we never did that.

We bought loose eggs that we put in a wicker basket and flour for chapattis that was placed in our own personal storage canister. There were very few prepackaged foods. Most of the items bought at the market were sold from huge wooden barrels or hessian bags, so it was not unusual to bring our own containers to carry the items in. The ice for the party was bought from the freezer shop by the kilo. Once we purchased a huge block of ice, it had to be chunked up into smaller pieces. By the time we arrived back at the beach house, it lost half of its mass, because it melted in the heat. The van left a water trail that quickly dried on the road. Once we got the block to the beach, I always liked trying to get pieces off with the ice pick. It was hard work, but it was fun, because it would cool me down.

By the time this particular party began, I was starving. I could hardly wait for the food to be cooked. While the adults were out in front of the beach house, I snuck into the kitchen and had my fill of beef curry. It was so good. Later when everyone began dinner, I wasn't hungry, because I had already eaten, but I ate some chicken korma just to make it look like I had not stolen food earlier. Afterward, I strolled up the beach to see if I could see any female turtles laying eggs, but I saw nothing. The moon was just a small sliver that resembled a skinny banana; it wasn't even shining that much. I turned back to the Dinosaur and settled myself comfortably on the back seat. I looked out the window and watched the moon disappear behind a cloud, and soon I fell asleep.

When I woke up the next day, I was back in bed at the Y. Malik probably had carried me in the night before, after the party ended. Later that day Mother and Jane had to go and film for the second commercial. I didn't want to go, and I opted to stay at the Y and play some chess with the old geezers.

After a few hours of beating everyone at chess, I started to get hungry. It was close to lunchtime anyway. I walked over to the window and noticed that a lone black chicken was pecking about out in the courtyard. I went to the cook and asked him in Urdu if he could make me a very mild chicken curry. He told me I would have to wait a while, but he would have it ready as soon as possible. I went and sat down at a table and watched the courtyard silently through the window. About a minute went by before I saw the headless black chicken running about. An hour later, I was eating my curry. By then, I was used to the idea of fresh food and its implications. I felt bad for eating something that had been alive and well an hour before, but I was really hungry, and I couldn't wait to tuck in. No guilt.

Soon after I ate, Mother returned with Malik. They wanted me to get cleaned up and ready to go with them to a dinner engagement that involved the filming crew. Jane was already with them, and we were to meet them at the home of one of the directors. I took a bath and put on my best dress. For the most part, I did not wear dresses unless it was for a photograph or a special occasion. I was somewhat of a tomboy myself by now, and I always wore pants, which had of late been falling about my waist. The zipper was always down, and I gained the charming nickname of Little Miss Open Fly. I hated it. Still, I dressed up and had my mother braid my hair and make me look nice. Servia had mentioned that he would soon be filming a tomato ketchup commercial in which they needed little girls. I figured that if I looked well groomed, I might be in a commercial like Jane.

We took a cab, because we thought the eyesore might not be such a great vehicle in which to drive up to a mansion. The Dinosaur still had shiny, bald tires, and to make matters worse, a few weeks earlier the muffler had fallen off in the middle of the street, making the van even noisier than before. Malik ran out of the van that day to retrieve the stupid thing and burnt his hand. This day, though, we were in a cab, going to meet some very important people.

We had not even driven ten minutes away from the Y when it suddenly down poured with rain. Within three minutes, water was up to the doors, and the cab stopped in the middle of the rapidly growing river. Children and adults alike started dancing in the rain, swimming around in the muddy water and having a blast. We left the cab to try and find a place to get out of the rain. Malik was carrying me so I would not get all dirty from the muddy water.

We were completely soaked from head to toe when we finally entered the lobby of a really massive five-star hotel. We stood in the entrance, and all of the people in the lobby turned their heads to stare. There was a look of disgust on everyone's face, but they soon went back to what they were doing. Malik took us up to the second floor, where there was a restaurant. We sat down at a table, and Malik went off to find us some towels.

There was a man sitting in front of us at another table who looked just how I had imagined my make-believe Afghani sheikh would. He had a long white gown on and a headpiece that came down over his shoulders with a black and gold cloth rope wrapped around his head like a crown. He opened a briefcase that we could see was filled with cash. This hotel was definitely for wealthy people. In fact, I had heard that one of Saudi Arabia's two thousand plus princes, was visiting Pakistan, and I figured that was him. Instantly I felt out of place and could not wait to get out of there.

The hotel had the best-running air conditioning on the planet, adding to my discomfort. At any other time, I would have paid for air conditioning that worked so well, but my mother and I were both soaked, and the cold made it really uncomfortable for us. My cotton dress was now stuck to my skin, and I was freezing cold. My neatly braided plaits now looked bedraggled and had pieces of hair sticking out in an untidy fashion. My mother felt even more self-conscious, as her blouse had also stuck to her, and she was wearing her hair out underneath a colorful scarf that was drenched. We looked and felt terrible. The whole ordeal was awful. I suddenly recalled how Beena had mentioned that the rain caused problems. She had not exaggerated!

About two minutes later, Malik came back with some small towels. That was all the hotel manager would give us. I thought that with all the money they made with their affluent guests, they could at least throw us a few large towels. Still, beggars can't be choosers, or so I had heard. We made adequate use of the small cloths. It was quite amazing how much a towel could absorb when you really needed it to. I started thinking of all the uses for a towel. Obviously, my mind was drifting. That had happened quite often lately. I actually found it rather amusing. I wanted to laugh but thought better of it. Then I felt like crying. I am not sure how long we were there or how exactly we left the hotel, but one fact I do remember is that we didn't get to go to the director's house that day. It was all very disappointing.

When we arrived back at the Y, Beena was raving on about how Mother had brought rain to them. She was dancing around with her palms facing the ceiling and her arms extended. Betty came over, soaking wet, and was also dancing about. He was overjoyed that it had finally rained. He came over to my mother and was thanking her. I just knew that something weird like that was going to happen. Everyone was so grateful to her. She made a lot of people happy. I was sure the Pakistani economy would be bolstered and the crops would now grow. Everybody was ecstatic that day except me, because my dress had been ruined, and we didn't get to eat dinner at the nice big mansion.

By the time the second commercial had been filmed, we had met several wealthy acquaintances at parties. We met people who were politicians, famous artists, high-ranking military officials, all kinds. There were people interested in Jane's work, and there were people interested in Mother. There were a few individuals, who liked me, but I was young, and I could not hang out in the same manner as Mother and Jane.

Still, I had a friend called Danny. He was a Pakistani pilot who talked to me and brought me presents. I was nowhere near fourteen, so

I knew he didn't want to marry me. I felt that he was a generally good man, and if he had any nasty thoughts about me, he never showed them. Mother knew him and had no problems with him, until one day when he took me to the Karachi international airport without her knowledge.

We went by rickshaw, a small, three-wheeled, open cab of sorts. Danny had a business meeting with some aviation personnel. He was really nice, and he introduced me to the other aviators and businessmen. He spoke in English the whole time. He was telling them about how I came to be there and how Mother, Jane, and I were living at the Y. It was a really pleasant day, but when we returned, Mother was furious with him. She wouldn't let me hang out with him again, because she was worried that he was a child molester or something. The truth was, though, he never laid a hand on me in any inappropriate way at all. I think he just saw a lonely kid and thought he would keep me company for the day. Still, I realize why Mother was overly concerned. After all, I knew I was not supposed to leave the premises, especially with a man.

The sad side of meeting all kinds of different people was that you could never tell what they were really like or what their true nature was. One would have to judge a person on gut instinct alone. My naïve philosophy was that everyone was nice unless proved otherwise. If someone was not physically harming me, then that person was a good guy. I probably learned this trait from my mother, who also had the proclivity to trust almost anyone. Emotional and sexual abuse was a concept I didn't recognize at this time in my life and fortunately was not an issue.

Obviously, the Y had mostly male lodgers, with all kinds of foreign men checking in and out on a daily basis. We met a lad who was visiting Pakistan for a vacation. He was only at the Y a few days, but we liked him because he was from Britain, and we had that in common. His name was Jack, so we gave him the nickname "Union Jack," because he was from England. One day, he asked my mother if she could drop him off at the airport, as he was taking a flight back home the next day. Being true to her obliging nature, she agreed.

We met up the next morning and waited for him to get to the van. He brought one suitcase down and put it in the back of the Dinosaur. While he was going in for his travel bag and last items, Malik and a customs guy we had met at the Y came running over, somewhat concerned. He said not to take Jack to the airport, as he had cocaine in his suitcase, and the customs guy knew that the police were waiting at the airport to grab him. He told her that if she took Jack, she could be in trouble as well. Mother was stupefied. There was no time to find out if the customs guy was telling the truth, so she grabbed the suitcase out of the back of the van and placed it on the side of the road. Just then, Union Jack was coming out of the Y. Mother told him that she was really sorry, but an emergency situation had turned up, and she could not take him to the airport. She hated lying but didn't know what else to say. It was not like she could just ask him right out, "Do you have cocaine in your suitcase?" Disappointed, Jack called for a cab. The next day, the local paper featured a small article on the capture of a British drug smuggler called Jack. Malik showed us the paper, but it was all Greek to us. Actually, it was Urdu, but either way, we could not read it. Apparently, Jack had filled two containers of baby powder with cocaine and was caught, just like the customs man had said. I was shocked that this seemingly nice guy had turned out to be a criminal. You just couldn't tell. Back in England, these types of things happened on TV, but now it was real. I was living a movie.

A few days later, the rain stopped, and the ground was back to its normal dry state. It didn't take long for the rain to seep away completely, but it did help while it was raining. Plants were actually looking greener after only a few days, and the grasses were perking up. Most importantly, the rain had cooled the air a couple of degrees. It didn't seem like it would make that much of a difference, but every degree counted once the temperature was above one hundred and ten.

Because it was not so sweltering outside, Malik took us out to eat at a restaurant called the Village. It was a neat place where tables were set in booths that were outside. The grounds were surrounded by a bamboo fence, and all the booths were sectioned off with the same bamboo and adorned with quaint cane-grass rooftops. It was clear why they called it the Village. Young women came around to the tables and sold beautiful-smelling jasmine flower necklaces or gardenia brooches. Sometimes they had roses and other aromatic flowers, but jasmine and gardenia were the most popular. Despite the seating being outside, the air always smelled fragrant because of the flowers the girls sold. The food was tasty and a good price, too. Soon, the Village became a favorite place to go.

For every good thing gained, there would have to be a downside, it seemed. A disturbing part of the outside restaurant was the rats. Occasionally, I would be tucking into a nice piece of chicken or drinking a cool glass of mango juice when suddenly out of the corner of my eye, I would catch a rat scurrying across the ground. Some of the clever ones ran along the edge of the fence and dropped down on your table to see if they could grab a quick meal. There were a lot of rodents, but if we didn't bother them, then they generally didn't bother us. Even though the grounds were rat infested, all manner of people went there, locals, tourists, and businessmen alike, and most often while there, Mother made another new friend.

A few days later, we were eating at the Village again. While we were there, Mother met a charming French-Vietnamese businessman called Noel. I liked Noel. He reminded me of my father, probably because his features were more Asian than French. I had not seen my father for several years. After Mother married Ryan, my father just gave up on us. I often thought about him and missed him, but it had been three years since I last saw him, and it hurt knowing that he didn't want to see me anymore. Mother told me that it was important for me to know that the people I was with were the ones who loved me, and that was all that mattered. I guess that was a standard parental pep talk, and my mother knew how to talk. Pep talk, sweet talk, friendly talk, whatever the talk was that became necessary, or was relevant for a situation; she knew how to talk it.

At this time, she was talking to Noel. I didn't actually ever listen very closely to adult conversation. Much of the time, I was oblivious to anything that was being said, but because I was interested in Noel, I did catch some words like he was on a business trip, he spoke about fifty languages, and he was going to Lahore in a couple of days for a business meeting. He was very charming, and he did have a sweet French accent. Every now and then, he said, "Ow are you doing, little girl?" or some words to that effect. He would smile at me and then return his gaze to Mother, and they would continue their boring conversation.

The fact was that I was interested only in food. It seemed like I was hungry all the time. Noel had commented on my eating habits, and Mother explained how I could only eat certain foods, so when I did find something that agreed with my stomach, I went all out. With that, he offered to take us the next evening to that classy Chinese restaurant that cost a fortune. I was ecstatic, and I hoped my mother would agree. She did, and the next evening, we were having the most delicious Chinese food on the face of the earth. Noel was so kind and really cool. He said that in a few days he would take us out again—as long as

Mother did the driving, he joked. We accepted the invitation with great enthusiasm. Noel said he would meet us at the Y in a few days' time.

The next few days were busy. We had been invited to everyone's place, it seemed. One of the acquaintances that requested our company was an artist called Mr. M. Turab. He painted the most wonderful pictures on huge canvasses, bigger than the average person's wall, and was delighted to show his work to my mother. We met his whole family and were often welcomed to their home. They invited us to stay with them for a couple of days. They had a huge house. The sleeping quarters were divided into two sections, one side for the males in the family and the other for females and children. In the middle was a large room for family meetings.

One day while we were there, one of Mr. Turab's many sons asked Jane and me to go and view his newly decorated room. He was excited because he had been allowed to paint his room a different color from the rest of the house, which was white. He used his father's talents against him by using the excuse of artistic expression as his reason for changing his room. The room was painted blue on all four walls and the ceiling, except he had left a four-inch white margin around all of the edges. There was matching blue carpet, and his bed was set at an angle in the middle of his room. Hanging aesthetically on the walls were a few of his father's smaller art renderings, in blue hues that matched the room. It looked very nice, and we understood why he was so enthusiastic about showing it off. Not two minutes went by before Jane and I were told to get out of that side of the house. The ladies laughed at us instead of punishing us for breaking the rules, which is what I fully expected. Because we were English, and our ways were different from their Muslim ways, they forgave us. I was glad they realized we were different, because I didn't want to get in trouble again.

After that brief encounter with the women, we went to an art gallery and saw some of Mr. Turab's work that he had for sale. He truly was a skilled artist, and I wished I could paint like him. One of his most fabulous paintings was of a Bengal tiger chasing down his prey. The details were astounding, and even though I was just a kid, the painting moved me. I was sad that the tiger was poised for a kill, but Mr. Turab told me that it was the circle of life, that if the tiger did not catch the prey, he would go hungry. It made sense in a macabre way. Mr. Turab was a wise soul. A person who can move a child through his art is truly an artist. I admired the old man.

Not everyone we met was an artist, director, or general. Many of our friends were average folk like us. We had met a friend of Servia's called Shahid back in June, through Jane's work. When Jane turned fourteen, Shahid and Servia organized a birthday party for her at Shahid's big apartment. Shahid and Jane had taken a liking to each other, and soon after, he started hanging out with us and was part of our group of friends. We met many people at the party at Shahid's. In fact, that was where we met Danny, the pilot who was forbidden to talk to me anymore because of the airport ordeal.

Servia also introduced us to his family. They lived about twenty miles out of Karachi, so we could not visit them very often, but one of the great things about Servia's family was that there were children of my age. Now and again, I was permitted to stay with them for a few days and play games and watch their black-and-white television. It was wonderful, because I could watch American TV shows. The only difficult part was trying to translate the dialogue into English. Three main languages were spoken here: Punjabi, Hindi, and Urdu. There were other dialects such as Sindi, but I learned only a few sentences in Urdu, and they mainly had to do with asking for food and water.

One of the girls in the family was two years older than me; her name was Kimi. She spoke enough English to translate for me, but that became tiring for her. She was also needed quite often in the kitchen, so I didn't always get to spend much time with her. Still, I played with the younger children, and that made me feel good. They didn't have many games or toys, but we made do with checkers and Snakes and Ladders. It always dragged to have to leave. It seemed like they lived so far away, but every chance I had to see them, I would take it, just to be with people my own age.

Chapter 12

Beggar Man, Thief

Back at the Y, Mother had made friends with a German couple, Caspar and Emelie. They wanted to take a break from university and get an education by traveling around for a while. We were used to meeting all types, and these two were really neat. I adored German accents and could listen to the sound all day. It was strange, because listening to them speaking in English with their German accent was cool, but when they spoke German, it seemed a bit harsh to the ears for me. They didn't speak German in front of me very often, so I didn't have to endure the sound all that much.

We started meeting them for breakfast and lunch, and we sat around in the Y cafeteria for hours, chatting with them. One day while Mother nattered to them, I went and had a game or two of chess with the old men. Caspar came over and challenged me to a couple of games; I was that good. He praised my technique, which made me feel happy. I was glad that I was good at something, because I had felt quite inadequate lately.

Soon after the chess games were over, it was time for lunch, but those plans were cut short by the arrival of Noel. He entered the cafeteria dressed immaculately, as usual. He always wore the best tailored silk suits and had his hair done so he would look dashing at all times. He was very charismatic, for sure. He had mentioned that he would stop by and take us out to the Chinese restaurant. Caspar, Emelie, and Noel were introduced to each other, and before long, everyone was in deep conversation, laughing and chattering as usual. Time went by pretty fast, and before long, I was starving again. I couldn't wait until dinnertime, which was fast approaching. Finally, Noel asked my mother if it was all right to invite Caspar and Emelie along for dinner. Mother didn't mind if they came along, if they wanted to. There was no doubt that we had enough room in the Dinosaur, as long as they could all tolerate the roar. A few jokes were made about the poor old Dinosaur, and then we were all on the way for Chinese food. One again, the food was exquisite. I couldn't have been happier. We had a nice evening with our newly found friends, and my belly was full of food that I enjoyed and could tolerate. I went to bed a happy kid that night.

We had now been at the Y for several months without a male in the family, and we were told that we might have to find somewhere else to stay. Mother received the divorce papers from Ryan, cruelly reminding us we were alone. It was quite evident by now he was not coming back to join us. So far, no new plans had been made to get us on a ship to Australia. For the moment, it looked like we would be staying in Karachi for a while. Malik set up a day to view apartments for rent. The first place we went to view was in a basement. As we entered the first room, we noticed it was kind of damp and smelled like mold. The owner flicked on the light, and with that, a large, black mass of mouse-sized roaches lurched toward Mother's full-length skirt. She let out a horrified scream and started dancing around like a madwoman. I thought it was hilarious. It reminded me of the time she was stomping around on the ants in Afghanistan. In retrospect, it was pretty gross. The roaches were trying to get out of the light and find somewhere to hide. The only available darkness was under my mother's skirt. Needless to say, we did not rent that place.

The next potential apartment was not too far away from the Y. Even though we had to leave, we wanted to be in close proximity, so we could still meet up with friends. We were told that we could go back there every day, but we couldn't stay there anymore, because of the rules of the Y. It didn't take long before we found a suitable place to stay. It was about six miles away from the Y but not within walking range, especially in the heat. The apartment was on the top floor of a very basic two-story building. It was a rectangle divided into four rooms in a row. There was a kitchen, two living spaces, and a bathroom. To get to it, we had one staircase leading to the front balcony that ran the length of the building. Each room had a door leading out to the balcony, which was roped off along the entire length. It looked like the side of a boat, so we called it the boathouse, even though it was nowhere near the ocean. Within a few days, we had moved in. Everyone we knew gave us pieces of furniture and household items. We took many of our belongings and cooking items from the van, and before long, we were well and truly settled in.

Kanji was devastated that we had to leave the Y, even though we moved only a few miles away. He was concerned that he wouldn't be able to walk that far to serve Mother. She assured him that it was okay and that we would be visiting the Y every day and would see him then. Besides, I had to go to see Kanji's wife every few days to get the lice pulled out of my hair. Nothing that we were doing was working to get rid of the pesky critters. One day, in order to eliminate half of the population of the lice, and not knowing what else to do, Mother cut my hair short. I was so unhappy. I hated the haircut, even though everyone said I looked nice. It was not true. I looked and felt horrible, and I could not wait for my hair to grow back. Even at the length it was, I still had to go back to Lata for regular grooming.

We didn't always stay in the boathouse. It had no air-conditioning, and it would get really hot. Shahid would let us stay in his huge apartment, which did have air conditioning, a luxury that we often craved to get relief from the intense heat. It was the same apartment where Jane's birthday party had been. While we were staying there for a few days, I started to feel pretty ill. Every time I ate, I felt hungrier but at the same time quite sick.

One afternoon I was napping in one of Shahid's guest rooms when I woke up suddenly with this urge to throw up. I went to the toilet and hurled up all my breakfast. I looked at the puke and did not remember eating noodles recently. It baffled me, so I went to fetch my mother, to show her that the noodles I had eaten a week ago were still in my stomach. When she looked in the toilet, she almost puked too. She flushed the offending food down the drain and marched me to the Y to find Kanji.

We could not find him, but we found Noel having lunch with Caspar and Emelie. Mother looked flustered, and Noel asked what was wrong. My mother told him about the dreaded vomit. I was feeling quite queasy and kind of worried because I didn't know what was wrong. After the conversation about the vomit was over, a new conversation arose about my hair. Noel had not seen it cut, and he asked why it was short. Once again, I was being discussed. Unlike the positive attention Jane received for her acting, I felt that my attention was not good at all.

When they finished talking about my hair, Noel demanded that we go to a pharmacy right away. He told Caspar and Emelie that we would meet them later and go for dinner. With that, we took off to the pharmacy, where Noel bought me a medicated shampoo for the lice in my hair and medicine for my upset stomach. I was told to take two types of pills for the nausea for several weeks and to make sure I did not miss a dose.

A few days later, when the sick feeling had passed and I was not puking up old food anymore, my mother felt that I could handle the truth about my stomach problems. She told me that it wasn't noodles that I had been throwing up; it was worms. She had been making regular potty checks to make sure that they were gone. I was unaware that worms came out from other parts of the body. I was never that interested to see what was in the loo after I was done with it. But once I knew that I had been harboring unwanted guests, I started taking more interest in what was leaving my body. I had picked up two types of parasitic roundworms that had been making me sick for months. All that hunger was because of those fat worms taking all my nutrition from inside my intestines; there were so many of them that they backed up into my stomach, where they died. That also explained the severe weight loss. I recalled that day at one of the beach parties when I was told not to eat the beef curry until it was thoroughly cooked. I figured I caught them from that. I had wondered why I was eating so much but my pants were falling off. Now I knew. It took a few days before I was feeling completely better, but Noel took care of me during this time. He paid a lot of attention to me and was constantly trying to ease my discomfort by spoiling me with gifts.

About a week after the pharmacy day, Noel took us out with Caspar and Emelie. Noel said he was treating us all to a meal at a restaurant in his hotel. Mother drove us all there, and we went in anticipating the food, which Noel had said was high quality. Noel ordered all the meals; it was a huge spread. The dishes that came out looked delicious. My appetite had decreased somewhat after the ordeal at Shahid's apartment, but I was told I must eat something. Noel had ordered me some light food and a few bottles of mango juice.

As we sat eating, Jane reached over to sample what looked like a really tasty dish that Caspar was eating. Noel just about had a cow and demanded that she not touch another person's food. He said that it was rude. Caspar said he didn't mind, but Noel was becoming enraged, so Jane backed down and ate what was on her own plate. We were all taken aback for a second, as we had never seen Noel behave in any manner but dignified.

A few minutes later, a few of Noel's acquaintances came out of nowhere. We didn't know them, and he did not introduce us to them, either. He moved to another table and sat there for ages, talking in what we thought was French. No one knew what he was saying, but we all knew we had upset him. We didn't mean to abuse his kindness, but we didn't know we were offending his Buddhist customs by wanting to try someone else's food. Caspar and Emelie were behaving strangely by now. They had kind of gone off their meals and didn't want to talk much. We felt so bad, especially Jane, who felt that she had been responsible for the whole ordeal. Caspar said that he did not feel well and wanted to return to the Y. With that, Noel jumped back into the conversation. By now, he had calmed down, and he was acting like his old, concerned self again. He asked Caspar what was wrong. Caspar told him he was just tired and wanted to go to sleep, as it was getting late. Noel offered to put them up for the night at his hotel. They agreed, and soon Noel was accompanying us to the front gates of the hotel. He apologized for his outburst, gave Mother some gas money, told us he would take care of Casper and Emelie, and requested that we meet him for breakfast the next day at the usual place.

The next morning, we met Noel in the Y cafeteria. He spent the whole day with us, buying Jane and I whatever we desired, and took us to eat at my favorite restaurant. He told us that Caspar and Emelie had taken ill overnight, and he was waiting to hear back from the doctor to find out what was wrong with them. I began thinking of a few sicknesses they might have: amoebic dysentery, gastrointestinal bacterial infection, or parasitic worms. I was becoming a real expert on common diseases and infestations of the area, since I was contracting everything humanly possible.

Every hour or so, Noel went off to a telephone booth to call his hotel. Finally, he must have found out what the doctor had prescribed, as he asked Mother if she could take him to a hotel where there was a pharmacy. Obviously, she wasn't going to refuse to help our friends. She felt awful that they had become sick, and Noel had already done so much for us.

The next place we went was a ritzy hotel. Noel took us in with him while he fetched the medicine. While we were there, he bought us even more treats. He was spending his money on anything we wanted. Jane and I had candy, big boxes of gum, books, a whole bunch of goodies. After a while, Mother had to ask us to stop seeing things we liked. We understood and quieted down. Noel was so generous. We had really found a knight in shining armor. I liked him so much and hoped he would be our friend forever.

Later that evening, we dropped him off at his hotel. He asked Jane to quickly help him with some of the bags he had bought from the other hotel, which was fine with Mother, because Jane wanted to make sure that Emelie and Caspar were okay. Mother and I waited in the van. We kept it running, and within about two minutes, Jane came skipping down the pathway and returned to the van. On the way back home, Mother asked how Caspar and Emelie were doing. Jane said that they were fine and resting comfortably in a room next to Noel. She also had a message from Noel to meet him at six the next morning at the Y.

The following day, we arrived at the Y a little after six AM. We waited in the parking lot, but Noel did not turn up. Mother went inside and asked the cafeteria staff if they had seen him, but they said he had not come in yet. They said it was odd that he wasn't there, because he had been turning up early every morning for the last few weeks to spend time with Caspar and Emelie. Mother was not aware that Noel had been visiting them so often. We knew that they had seen each other once in a while, but not every day. We had been busy moving to the boathouse and resting at Shahid's for a few days, so there was no way we could have known how much time he was spending with them. Still, we were all friends, so she saw no harm in him hanging out with them.

We decided to sit in the cafeteria and wait for Noel to turn up. He was not usually late for appointments, and Mother wondered if he had forgotten he had told us to meet him. While we were waiting, one of the lodgers came over and asked where our friend was. We had many friends, so it was unclear which one he was referring to. He asked again, mentioning the Frenchman. We knew then that he meant Noel. We told him that we didn't know where he was and that we were waiting for him too. He skulked off with an angry look on his face.

After about fifteen minutes, Kanji ran into the cafeteria. He was frantic and waving his arms about in a panicked manner. He ran over and told Mother to go now, to escape while she could. Confused, she asked Kanji to calm down and explain what was going on. He told us that Interpol was looking for her. She tried to calm him, explaining that we didn't need to escape from Interpol, and she asked him what it was about. Kanji didn't know exactly what was going on either. He was just concerned, and he thought we were in trouble.

A few minutes later, policemen from Interpol walked into the cafeteria and approached us for questioning. They said we had to go with them to the local police station, and we were advised to comply without incident. Mother asked them what was going on, but they said they could not discuss it at that location. Knowing how Mother didn't like to do anything she didn't want to do, I was concerned that she might have a sudden indignant outburst, but instead she was calmly reserved. Soon we were on our way out the door, accompanied by eight Interpol policemen.

When we arrived at the police station, Mother and I were ushered into a large room that was divided into jail cells with bars. Again, Mother asked what all the fuss was about. I was a bit worried, and I wondered if I had done something stupid. In South Asia anything could be considered an offense. One could get in trouble for a lot of weird and unusual things. Stomping on insects, touching dogs and cats, even going to the wrong side of a building could get you in trouble, so I was not sure exactly what had occurred. Maybe the van had been making too much noise without its muffler, I was not certain, but when I saw the cells, I thought we were going to be locked up. On closer inspection, I saw that they were not being used for imprisonment, but instead as temporary evidence chambers. We still didn't know what we were doing there.

The inspector opened each cell, one by one, and asked Mother to have a good look at the items laid out and tell them if she recognized anything. In the first cage, there were cameras, silver hardcover suitcases, black travel bags, jewelry, clothing, sunglasses, loose gems, passports, and foreign currency of all denominations. It reminded me of items I had seen in a James Bond movie. Mother looked over the mass of items and shook her head. She did not recognize anything there. The cash was definitely something we didn't recognize. We had been so broke lately that we were almost beggars at this point, and any money would have been nice to identify as ours, but it wasn't, so on we went.

The second cage had similar suitcases that were laid open for the contents to be viewed. In them were more than a hundred bottles of different prescription drugs, syringes, cubes of hashish, and other paraphernalia. Once I saw the drugs, it occurred to me that maybe this had something to do with Union Jack, until I saw something that troubled me. Two of the black travel bags with medicine in them looked very similar to the bags that Noel had bought at the big hotel, but I didn't say anything. Lots of people had those types of travel bags. I scooted in closer to Mother's side. The situation was becoming unnerving.

Mother just stared at the suitcases and shook her head, most likely in disbelief. She had obviously noticed that some of this stuff looked similar to Noel's, and she could not come to terms with it. When the inspector saw her shaking her head, he moved us on to the next cage for the last viewing. On a table lay several handguns, knives, rifles, and other weapons that I had no name for. They were all tagged with tiny pieces of paper hanging from string. Some of the guns were in plastic bags, and some were not. There were also boxes of handgun bullets and bigger ammunition. Mother told the police officer that she had certainly not seen any of these items before. I knew I had not seen any weapons. Ever since a rifle had been put to my skull at the Pakistan border, I had become intensely fearful of any type of projectile weapon; even a homemade slingshot made me nervous.

After the viewing, we were led out to a desk where we were asked to sit down. The inspector did not look at me once; he kept his gaze on Mother's eyes. He asked her a series of questions, reading her face at every answer. There were countless inquiries regarding Noel and the dynamics of his relationship to us. I could tell that Mother was distraught, but she kept calm and answered all the questions directly and honestly. Every time she answered, he scribbled notes in a large notebook and then went back to delve into the mind behind Mother's face. He didn't change his expression the whole time. It was spooky, like he was a robot, without feeling. I think he was supposed to be a human lie detector or something. The jailhouse itself was pretty shabby, so they probably couldn't afford a polygraph machine. I knew by then that there was something wrong here that undeniably involved Noel. I wanted to believe that my hero had been mistaken for someone else, but it was becoming quite clear that he was not the man I thought he was. After the last question was answered, the inspector wrote something down and closed his book. He gave Mother a stunted grin and thanked her for her honesty. He then explained the situation.

Noel was a wanted criminal in several countries. For years he had managed to evade the authorities and avoid imprisonment. Interpol had been following his trail month after month, always missing the opportunity to catch him at the last minute. He had many aliases, including the familiar Noel Benois. We didn't know his true identity until we were called in for questioning. Knowing his real name didn't tell us anything about his true nature. A few details from a list of crimes were disclosed, giving us an idea of whom we had been spending the last few weeks with.

Interpol believed that Noel had dealt in theft, weapons sales, and murder, among other things. Without physically capturing him, there was no proof that Noel was linked to their evidence. Supposedly, when his small-time arms dealings and theft jobs dwindled, he found other ways to make cash. Finding affluent couples and befriending them to procure items of potential value was one means of making ready money. After slowly poisoning the innocent victims over a series of days, he would pretend to help by having them moved close to him, where so-called doctors were available around the clock. Once a diagnosis was made, he would then run to a pharmacy to get medicine and administer it to the unsuspecting patients. While moving the sick victims to his hotel or lodgings, he would take their already-packed belongings to his room, where he would search through and take all the valuable items, including money, jewelry, expensive electronics, and travel documents, while the couple lay unconscious in the place of his choice. After completely pillaging their goods, he would administer fatal doses of poison. Soon after, he would board an already-booked flight out of the country and begin all over again somewhere else in the world. The passports he procured from victims were altered, with his photograph replacing that of the holder. He used the altered passports to flee the countries where he had committed crimes. As soon as he arrived in a new country, he ditched the passport and used another for a new temporary identity. This was how he avoided capture. It was very efficient.

Noel frequently befriended couples to divert suspicion from his intended exploits. He took his time preparing his plan by carefully picking out innocent characters he could use to aid in his nefarious dealings. He made friends quickly, treated them well (with the cash he had stolen from someone else) to gain their trust, and kindly manipulated them into serving his purpose without a thread of suspicion from his new friends. Once his goal was achieved and he had fled the country, anyone who was questioned in connection with his actions or whereabouts honestly could not provide any information on him. There was never any real evidence to which they could testify, because they were completely oblivious to what was really happening. Thus, enter a single mother with two young daughters and a handy vehicle. Seeing as Noel was usually into large-scale money-making, I figured he killed people as a kind of pastime, a game of sorts. He played everyone like they were on a chessboard, and I was glad we appeared to be on his side. I wondered if he played chess for real and thought that he would make a really good opponent.

After the interview, Interpol took us along with the local police to the Karachi docks to see if we could find Noel amongst the passengers boarding various ships. He was nowhere to be seen. We were told not to leave the country until they gave us permission, not that we were going anywhere in a hurry anyway. After we had searched the docks, Interpol took us back to the Y. Later that day we were told that Noel had been traced as having left on the previous night's flight to Bangkok under an alias. Our involvement ended there, and the local police and Interpol were satisfied that we had no connection to the crimes that Noel had committed.

The day before, Noel had asked Mother if she would drive him to Lahore for a business trip. We were supposed to meet him at the Y at noon. We found out that Noel initially had booked his flight, under Caspar's name, to leave two days later. Interpol believed that he had not expected anyone to visit Emelie and Caspar, so when Jane went to see how they were, Noel panicked, thinking that she would tell Mother that they were comatose. But Jane didn't recognize them as being comatose; she thought they were sleeping soundly. He canceled the usual evening dinner and staged a meeting for six the next morning. A few hours after we last saw him, he left the country.

After we had dropped him off at the hotel that night he had the food fit, Noel had returned to the Y and entered Emelie and Caspar's room with a key that he had stolen from them while they were unconscious. He told the receptionist at the Y that Emelie had sent him there to get their belongings. Because everyone had seen them together constantly for weeks, the receptionist had no idea what Noel was up to. He allowed Noel to go to their room, where Noel proceeded to take everything. He left a few hours later.

That night, by chance, Emelie and Caspar were found near death. An ambulance and the police were called, and they were rushed to the hospital, where Emelie quickly regained consciousness. She could barely speak, but she mentioned the few names she could, which included Noel, Mother, and a few others who had been pawns in Noel's game. The method in which the crime had been staged quickly alerted Interpol to the scene, where they found out that their much-wanted criminal had struck again. The police found some items left by Noel in the adjoining room, one of which was a copy of *The French Connection*.

Even after hearing all this disturbing news about Noel, I didn't want to believe he had really been doing these things. It was almost as disappointing as hearing that my father no longer wanted to see me, or realizing that Ryan had abandoned us. I was heartbroken. I was learning extremely negative lessons about trust.

Mother had to deal with her own trust issues. Her first reaction to hearing what Caspar and Emelie were going through was that of concern. She was appalled and upset to hear that they were near death, and she wanted to be near their side to provide support. When they were first admitted to the hospital, the police did not permit us to see them, but when Emelie gained awareness, she requested that we not be allowed near either of them. Emelie thought that we had known what Noel was doing. This hurt Mother tremendously. She cried constantly for days. It was difficult to see her so emotionally distraught, as Mother usually was so strong. Nothing swayed her, but this was different. Of all the traumatic experiences we had suffered, this outwardly affected her the most.

By the time we returned to the Y, everyone knew what had happened with Noel. Word had already spread to the local news, and it was distributed over the radio and in newspapers. Some people doubted us now, and we were looked on with suspicion by many of the folks we had lived with and considered friends. Kanji and a few of the permanent staff were still as faithful as ever, knowing that Mother might be a strange character but was not a co-conspirator to theft and attempted murder. Obviously, she was glad that they believed in her, but the idea that Emelie didn't trust her tore Mother apart. Caspar was in the hospital for days. He was still very sick when his family flew him and Emelie back to Germany a week later.

Several days before they left, Mother confronted Emelie in the Y cafeteria. Mother apologized from her heart for what had happened. Emelie could barely look up at her, but eventually she raised her head and said it was all right. Clearly it was not all right, but what else could be said? Eventually, Mother came to terms with the fact that no matter how innocently she had contributed to their misfortune, she was a factor nonetheless. She recognized why Emelie had a problem with it, but a few days later, Emelie talked to Mother again. Emelie said that she realized that Noel was no more a friend to us than he had been to them. It had become clear to her that befriending a mother and her children made it look as though he was a true gentleman. She saw how he had used us to present the illusion and hide the evil, which enabled him to gain their trust.

After Emelie and Caspar left, we were still very saddened by the events that led up to their departure, and to make matters worse, we never found out if Caspar recovered fully. Looking back on the days leading up to the morning Interpol had confronted us, Mother speculated that Noel might have intended to dispose of us on the business trip to Lahore, before coming back and finishing off our friends. It might have been Jane's concern for Emelie and Caspar that saved us all from a deadly end.

Chapter 13

Forgive and Forget

After several weeks had gone by, the atmosphere at the Y began to take on a more familiar feeling. As sad as it was, the story of Emelie and Caspar's tragedy was passing. People started talking about other subjects again. As previous boarders left, new ones arrived. It was not long before we were making new friends once more.

One friend was a woman named Elizabeth who preferred to be called Beth. She was from England, and she was staying at the Y with her companion. They had been backpacking their way around Europe and the Middle East. Unfortunately, Beth's man took off with a Swedish girl and left her at the Y for days before she realized what had happened. She contemplated going back to England, but she decided that she would make the most of it and continue touring Pakistan for a while. Mother and Beth talked for hours, laughing and joking into the wee hours of the night as they shared stories. I guess they had quite a lot in common, including their name. Mother had always liked to be called Elizabeth by others, but Malik had started calling her Elli back when they met, and the nickname had stuck to her. Anyway, Beth and my mother really clicked. It was good to see that she could laugh and joke again after the horrible ordeal with Noel, Emelie, and Caspar.

In addition to keeping company with new acquaintances, we were still in touch with old friends. Servia was still very much involved with us, and he had been making arrangements for two more commercials to be filmed, which we desperately needed, as we were running out of money. The money from Jane's commercial had helped us to survive for a little while, as it was inexpensive to live in Pakistan, but we needed more now. The first job was a cereal commercial that Mother, Jane, and I were going to be in, and the other was the tomato ketchup commercial that I had wanted to be in for what seemed like months. Other children my age were going to be in the advertisement too. All I wanted to know was if any of them spoke English, as I was desperate to play with children of my age that I could understand.

While we were waiting for word on the progress of that development, it was time to view Jane's second commercial, for United Paints, in the cinema. I wondered whether we would stay to see the film this time, or if Jane would want to leave in a panic. Once again, the huge screen lit up. The anticipation of seeing Jane up there for a second time was killing me. Eventually, the commercial came on, and all the familiar feelings came over me. It was just so awesome to see Jane up there, looking so professional and glamorous. Shortly after the viewing, we left. I don't even remember what the film was going to be. Still, I didn't care about that, because I was looking forward to the next day, as we were going on a day trip with Malik.

Malik was a constant part of our circle of friends, but recently he had been promoted at his work, and he didn't see as much of us as we would have liked. When he could, he took us for lunch or to the park. He found joy in showing us all the places that were going to be influenced by the bank he worked for. It was part of his new job, making decisions to finance new industry and commercial property in a big way. The world of business and tourism was expanding in Karachi, and the long-term goals were to improve the city of Karachi in a modern way while still keeping the history and heritage intact. Malik delighted in the fact that he could influence the conservation of park areas and wildlife while at the same time contributing his knowledge of business and tourism in commercial terms. One day, he took us to a huge walled-off area a few miles away from the boathouse. It was basically a huge, dry area of land that had a few saplings wilting in the intense heat. He told us all the details of the construction and development of this park and how in two years we would see a miracle light up this area. He was excited and driven when it came to his job, and I understood why job security was extremely important in Pakistan.

One early afternoon, we were having lunch with Beth at the Y cafeteria as usual when a frenzied Kanji came running up to Mother. Lata had finally gone into labor. Kanji wanted us to drive her to the hospital, and Lata wanted Mother to be with her at the birth. Beth, Mother, and I all started running to get the van ready. A few minutes later, Lata came waddling out, accompanied by Kanji. He looked terrified. I couldn't believe he was behaving so worried when this was to be their eleventh child. I thought that he would have been used to that situation by now.

When we arrived at the hospital, I had to wait outside in the van with Beth. Out of boredom, I asked how they were going to get the baby out of Lata's belly. She told me all the sordid details of how a newborn gets out of what I learned was a place called a uterus. She did weird demonstrations with an elastic band to visually demonstrate the whole procedure. It was all very fascinating and quite gross. I was not sure whether to ask my mother if it was true, because she had never talked to me about such things. So I took it for what it was and never pursued a conversation like that again. Finally, we heard news that the baby had been born. Kanji was overjoyed, and a few days later, they had a big celebration at his home.

It was November by now, exactly eight months since we had left England. It seemed like we were firmly based in Karachi, as our lives continued on. Australia hadn't been mentioned for months. None of our extended family appeared concerned that we had not shown up in Perth, and after our grandmother heard that Mother and Ryan had divorced, she went back to England. Even though the whole trip was a learning experience and a life-changing one at that, I started thinking about going back to school. Mother had been so preoccupied with trying to make ends meet, managing Jane's career, and dealing with Interpol that school had not crossed her mind.

Several issues had to be confronted. Exactly how long would we be there? What was Jane's future going to be? In general, what were we going to end up doing? At this point, anything was possible. We were not held down by the constraints of mediocre routine. Mother liked spontaneity, freedom, and the ability to choose what she wanted to do in life without being told it was wrong or unacceptable. We had lived the last few months like this. What we gained as free spirits, we lacked in other areas: the security of permanence and the benefits of proper nutrition, health care, and, for Jane and me, a formal education. These issues had to be addressed, and my mother had to make a decision.

We weighed the positive and negative aspects of our lives and considered everyone's views. For Mother, it was mostly good for her to stay. She loved Karachi, and she was unfettered, as she liked to be. She had friends, and she was enjoying being Jane's manager. On the negative side, money was a problem. We had enough to survive, and that was just about it. Jane had mixed feelings too. She liked being a model and had made many close friends. If anything, she may have felt that she was not living up to her full potential. Going back to

England and completing her education was a factor, but she had also become quite comfortable with the fancy-free lifestyle and her modeling career. As for me, I wanted to go surfing, swimming, and sunbathing on a beach in Australia, but as the question pertained to whether or not we should return to England, my response was absolutely yes. I had experienced lice in my hair, worms coming out of every orifice, amoebic and bacterial infections, and several pounds of weight loss. I had no close friends, I missed Katie, and I wanted to go back to school and maybe even continue pursuing my dream and become an Olympic gold medalist in figure skating.

With Christmas advancing on us and with the state of our personal matters, my mother decided that we should give up our vision of living in Australia and head back to England. There seemed no way that we could successfully exist, living in Pakistan. Deciding how we should return was daunting. Would we try to make it back the same way as we came, or would we try an alternate route? Would we take Beth with us, as she also desired to return to England, or would she stay? Unlike the trip out here, we didn't have the funding or resources to fully equip the van with all the provisions we would need for the long trip back. The tires looked like inflated inner tubes, and the muffler still had not been repaired. Beth and Mother discussed the matter, and they reached a compromise. Beth still wanted to travel, and she agreed to buy new tires and fix up the Dinosaur enough to travel in exchange for borrowing it. She would meet us back in England two months later and return the van to us. With assurances from Beth that she would be fine with those arrangements, the deal was done.

Chapter 14

Farewell to Alms

Mother decided it would be better if we just took a flight back to London. She sold her remaining two items of jewelry, which my father had bought her in Singapore several years before, and bought airline tickets. Soon, we were trying to organize everything for our airplane trip back. It was not as simple as one would have thought. We had quite a few belongings. Apart from the mass of luggage from the van, we had accumulated furniture and household items for the boathouse. It was proving to be much harder to leave our home than we had thought. I looked out from the balcony of our boathouse at all the other houses and people in our town and realized that I might never see it again. I knew that I would not get to shoo the tail-dropping lizards out of the house, throw scraps of food to the wild dogs and cats that lived around us, or walk on a crab-infested beach at night again. Those were some of the experiences that made this place special to me.

As we packed our suitcases, which had limited space, boxes of our belongings that we could not fit in were piling up. We gave most of the furniture to Kanji, and the remaining items went to neighbors. I had a big box of toys that I could not fit in my luggage, no matter what. I made sure I kept my red journal, Camel Merlin (as he was small), and my mouse, Wumsey. I would keep them as carry-on items.

The next day, we went to say our good-byes to Servia and his family. We took the box of toys, which now included Mother's two koala bears, and gave them to the children. I was sad to part with my toys, but I felt that they had gone to a good place. Kimi and her siblings deserved them. Servia was very upset that we had to leave. He had become a close friend and colleague. He had opened the door to modeling for Jane and turned her into the first girl ever to make moving color commercials in Pakistan. It felt like a great loss for everyone.

Malik was equally upset when we told him we were leaving. He understood, and he even went so far as to say that if it were not for his important job, he would have liked to come back with us. But Pakistan was his life, and we all knew he could not give up his extremely important career just because he missed the company of a few British girls.

The day we left, we were permitted to stay one last night at the Y, for old time's sake, I suppose. It was by far the most heartbreaking event ever. Everyone we knew came to say good-bye. Beena came and hugged Mother. She said that Mother's strength had given her strength. She had discussed her engagement with her family, and although initially they were not thrilled about the idea, they allowed her to break off the arranged engagement and marry the man she loved. That was a rare occurrence, but her family wanted her to be happy. Beena was extremely grateful for the friendship that she and Mother had.

Betty came floating in with his best *chalwar* on. He wrapped his arms around Mother and told her that he would miss her more than anyone he had ever met. He said we had been the greatest girlfriends he had ever had. He gave quick hugs to Jane and me, and with tears in his eyes, he made a melodramatic exit, whimpering as he scurried out of the family room, his scarf flowing behind him.

Iqbar and many of the old geezers came through from the game room and shook my hand good-bye. They said I was one of the best chess players they had. Hearing that from them made me feel happy and sad at the same time.

Pretty much everyone we had met at the Y came to say good-bye, except Kanji. It was getting close to the time when we had to leave. Mother asked Jane to run around to the other side of the building to fetch him, but he was nowhere to be found. She was really concerned, because Kanji had been a faithful servant and friend, and he was nowhere to be seen. Thirty minutes went by, and the taxi was waiting to take us to the airport. Sadly, we started to load into the cab. We were looking out of the window, still searching for a glimpse of Kanji, but we figured our good-byes to him and his family the evening before must have been the final farewell.

Just as Mother was opening the door to get into the taxi, Kanji flew out of nowhere and knelt before Mother's feet. He was crying profusely, saying that he was going to miss her so much. She raised him to his feet and put her arms around him. At first he pushed back, stating that she was too special for him to embrace her in such a way.

She pulled him closer and told him that was nonsense. With that, he fell into her arms like a child. I could not believe an old man could feel such sorrow. Before long, we were all in tears. Malik was trying very hard not to break down himself, but he told us that we had to move on. With that, Kanji turned away and sped off into the shelter of the Y.

When we arrived at the Pakistan international airport, I was excited, apprehensive, and somewhat scared. Malik hugged us all and said his good-byes. It was a very sad time. Shahid, who had become close friends with Jane, also came to say good-bye. After a very emotional farewell, we walked onto the airplane. It was a jumbo jet like the one I had thought we would fly to Australia in.

As we sat in our seats in anticipation of takeoff, I opened my little red book and noticed how little I had written after passing through Iran. I read through a few of the last entries. They were all undated.

We were chased by drug dealers today I was really scared

Ma told off a big General today

We went back to the General he had shaved his head bald. My legs are still shaking

Jane and I were almost shot by bandits. I was going to throw up, but I could not

We all went swimming in a little swimming pool. It was fun

All of us are really sick. Ryan won't get out of bed

Jane has been asked to do a real live commercial

Today I was told off for touching puppies

I saw a man climbing a mango tree with no shoes on he was throwing wild mangoes down on the ground

Found out Ryan has gone back to England without us

Had really good eggs for breakfast

Rode on a camel like a real jockey

There were many more one-line entries that pertained to certain situations I had experienced over the months. After reading the last entry, I asked Jane for a pen. I wrote my final entry for that journal.

December 18, 1975

We never made it to Australia.

As we took off, I had a gut-wrenching feeling that it was a mistake to leave. I started doubting our decision. My mother and Jane were crying. I felt bad, like perhaps it was my fault that they were unhappy. If I had not had so many problems, maybe we would have stayed, and our lives would have been fine. I started missing everybody already. I began thinking that I would never get to play chess with Iqbar again, never watch TV with Kimi and her brothers and sisters. I would not get to sit with Lata or hold her baby. Malik would no longer be there to take us out to cool places, and we would never see the miracle transformation of the park he showed us. I would never get to dance with Betty, or hear Beena's voice, or have the opportunity to ride a camel on the beach, or see crabs or huge sea turtles again.

There were so many things I would miss. I could not bear to think of everything we had been through. One of the worse feelings was recalling Noel, Emelie, and Caspar. I wanted to believe that Noel truly liked us for who we were and not because we were pawns in his horrific game. I wanted Emelie and Caspar to know that we honestly had nothing to do with what happened to them. I really liked them both and hoped that Caspar had recovered. It was all too much. I closed my eyes to think of something that would make me feel happy.

Chapter 15

Home Is Where You Hang Your Hat

I had fallen asleep and missed half the flight. I woke up when dinner was being served. My mother and Jane were still red-eyed from crying. The air hostess gave us our meals, and we began eating. During most of the flight, not much was said. After several hours of silence, we were flying over London.

I looked out of the window and saw a miniature aerial view of the River Thames, Big Ben, London Bridge, and the Houses of Parliament as we came in for a landing. Water was running sideways on the tiny, round airplane window; it was raining. I thought it looked like tears, probably because of how we all felt. It was pretty dismal outside, overcast and cloudy. We landed with a slight thud, and soon we were taxiing up to the terminal. As we exited the airplane, the smell of the cold English air filled my nostrils. It was so different from where we had come from that I had almost forgotten what cold smelled like.

When we reached the other side of the terminal, we saw Nan standing there, waiting for us. We went up to her and gave her a huge group hug. It was good to see family. I was holding Wumsey, the mouse that she had given to me, under my arm. His pink ears were bent, and his white fur almost matched his gray fur. The felt smile had come away from his face and turned almost upside down, giving him a pathetic, sad look. The petals on the daisy that was still firmly attached to his paw were discolored and wilted.

In my hand, I held Camel Merlin tightly. I could feel the coldness of his brass body inside my hand. I felt bad because we never had returned Wumsey to Australia, and now Camel Merlin had to live in the cold. We had spent almost seven months in Pakistan; it was our home, but now we were back in foggy old England. This was to be home now, because this was where we were. I realized that home just meant where you were at the time. That reminded me of the saying,

"Home is where you hang your hat." That was so true, and now I would be hanging my denim fishing hat on the back of an old chair or something else, instead of wearing it to protect my brain from the sun.

On the drive back to Bristol, I began recalling all the countries we had visited, the different places we had seen, and the many people we had met. My mother had been correct when she said we would have a thrilling trip, an education, and excitement. I had experienced it all and so much more, including treacherous mountain passes, near-death situations, and criminal acquaintances. The experiences were positive and negative. I had learned to accept and respect all people, no matter where they come from, what their social status was, or what religious beliefs they possessed. I had come to understand the meaning of friendships and the importance of trust. I had learned that an act of kindness could go a long way. I had become aware of my surroundings and the beauty of past and present times. Words like geography, botany, zoology, architecture, history, anthropology, politics, religion now all had meaning.

Over the next few months, we received letters and cards from a number of the people we had met on our travels. Shahid wrote to Jane on a regular basis, and Malik wrote to my mother. Occasionally, I also received a note or two from him. One of Malik's letters to me went as follows:

Lahore

Dear Jenny,

Thanks for the loving card you sent me at my birthday. Dear, I don't know when your birthday is, but anyhow you tell me what you want for Christmas. I hope it won't be a kitten or puppy. How is your school, are you studying well, what classes are you in? I know you are very happy there in England, but tell me, Jenny, do you miss me or not? Jenny dear, if I come over, will you again fight with me? I hope the answer is no, isn't it.

Jenny dear, I am sure you have developed your swimming more, especially under water, but look at me, I can't even swim an inch! Ha ha. How is your skating, are you going for it again or not? You know, Jenny, I have a brand-new motorcycle now. It is very fast. I wish I can give a ride to your Mum and you.

I think that Jane will be nice with you and you have also stopped complaining about her to your Mum. Mum and Jane love you very much so be nice with them and don't annoy your Mum, as if you do, but still being elder to you I have to say something.

Now, dear, I am ending this letter because I don't know what else to write, but before I finish writing, tell your Mum that don't worry Malik will come, and tell her he is still very good friend. OK.

Now dear Jenny I end this with all my best wishes and happiness in your life and May God bless you with long life.

Love your Malik

P.S. Pay my love to Jane and your Mum.

I thought it strange that Malik mentioned me fighting with him, because I didn't recall being angry at him except for when he would not give the beggars money. Still, I was happy he wrote to me.

Faith and Patrick kept in touch and visited us for a few days in Bristol. We reminisced about the time we had spent together in Iran, Afghanistan, and Pakistan. They had photographs of the trip, which were a blast to look at. Seeing their pictures authenticated a time that was becoming more like a dream than a real-life experience. They had lost contact with Keith, but they said they had left him content in India, where he said his destiny was. Faith and Patrick had just bought a brand-new Land Rover and were planning another trip that would take them back through India. They were making bets on whether Keith would still be there. While on the subject of India, we began talking about the Sothebys and how none of us had ever heard back from them, despite our attempts to make contact. That was rather upsetting, as we had no idea what became of them. I had my suspicions that they might have gone down in the Khyber Pass, but I never expressed my thoughts, because I didn't want it to be true.

We heard from Ali Khan, the car driver in Pakistan, who wrote that his wife had returned to him, and everything was fine with his family. We were happy, as that whole ordeal had been awful for him. He told us that whenever we wanted to go back and see him, his door was open, and that he would definitely take us on those tours he'd promised. Ali also told us that while driving a new car to a client, he had seen our Volkswagen dead down the side of an Afghanistan mountain. It had been stripped of everything, and all that remained was a carcass, a familiar sight out there. At the time there was no mention of the owners or driver of the vehicle, and he had feared the worst, so Ali was happy when he heard from us and that we were all well.

Mother contacted the British consulate to see if anyone had heard from Beth, but they had no alert out for her. No forwarding address that we were given for England panned out, and we never heard anything about her again. We had three missing comrades, and that wasn't good, as we knew full well that any threat in the rugged terrain of South Asia was real. I wanted to believe that everyone was alive and well, and that through the disappointments and dangers, everyone and everything was going to be okay. Maybe having faith would prove to be all I needed. I prayed to the one god that I believed presided over all people to give strength and good fortune to all our friends, to protect the Sothebys and Beth, and for us to start our new life back in England.

Although leaving Karachi was a poignant affair, there will never be a day when I'll regret the experiences I had. Through all the ups and downs, I met a wonderful array of people from different cultures, some away from their own countries and many on their home soil, and even though we didn't make it to Australia, it was a fantastic journey, and it was a privilege to have traveled across so many borders. The experience opened my eyes wider than I ever could have imagined. It broadened my mind and laid down a foundation that would allow me to be open-minded in all aspects of my life.

My mother's decision to move to Australia may not have panned out, regardless of all the detailed planning, but the act caused a domino effect of events that changed not only my perception of life, but also those of others, even if only in a small way.

www.ingramcontent.com/pod-product-compliance
Lightning Source LLC
Chambersburg PA
CBHW031318040426
42443CB00005B/122